Unlimited

Lewis Raymond Taylor is co-founder and CEO of The Coaching Masters, a programme which trains others to become life coaches. Having overcome years of hardship and adversity, from addiction to prison, he is now an accredited coaching trainer and business coach. He earned his PhD in Transformation Education Management from the Swiss School of Business Research. Lewis is a highly acclaimed keynote speaker and his life story was the subject of the Netflix documentary 'The Psychopath Life Coach'.

Unlimited

Turn Your Adversity into an Asset

LEWIS RAYMOND TAYLOR

PENGUIN LIFE

AN IMPRINT OF

PENGUIN BOOKS

PENGUIN LIFE

UK | USA | Canada | Ireland | Australia
India | New Zealand | South Africa

Penguin Life is part of the Penguin Random House group of companies
whose addresses can be found at global.penguinrandomhouse.com

Penguin Random House UK,
One Embassy Gardens, 8 Viaduct Gardens, London SW11 7BW

penguin.co.uk

First published 2026
001

Set in 13.2/16 pt Garamond Premier Pro
Typeset by Six Red Marbles UK, Thetford, Norfolk
Printed and bound in Great Britain by Clays Ltd, Elcograf S.p.A.

The authorized representative in the EEA is Penguin Random House Ireland,
Morrison Chambers, 32 Nassau Street, Dublin D02 YH68

A CIP catalogue record for this book is available from the British Library

ISBN: 978-0-241-64683-0

Contents

A Heads-Up

This book is real. Raw. And at times, heavy.

We'll be diving into things like violence, addiction, trauma, mental health, loss, self-harm and suicide. I won't sugar-coat any of it.

So, if it hits too hard at any point, take a break. Breathe. Reach out to someone you trust – a friend, a therapist, a professional. This book isn't a substitute for support. It's not meant to push you through the pain. It's here to help you find your own kind of strength, on your terms.

This book might shift the way you see things. Maybe even the way you see yourself. But go at your own pace.

There's no right way to do this – just *your* way.

Wherever you're starting from, it's okay.

And, however you get there, it's enough.

You've got this. *I promise.*

Preface: A Black Dot

'You're a buffoon!' The word was spat from my dad's mouth, the smell of vodka on his breath. It's an odd word, really. Not the sort you'll hear often in an argument in a pub car park. But something about the way he said it – the utter disdain, the force he threw it at me with – made my blood run cold.

Throughout my childhood, he'd get home from a long day at work, start drinking, and at some point the criticism would begin. I was bad at this. I was stupid for doing that. I would never amount to anything. He would smash his fist against the wall for emphasis as I flinched.

I was eight years old, and here was the one man I most needed to protect me in the world telling me I was worthless.

He used a lot of different words over the years, but for some reason that's the word that always echoed in my head. Still does.

Buffoon.

Every time I did something wrong – and for the first twenty-five years of my life that was pretty much all the time – I was proving him right. I was a clown. An idiot. I didn't have a clue what I was doing. I would literally hear his voice in my head saying it. I would see his face snarling at me. A reminder of all the things I couldn't do. Of all the things I didn't know. Of the disappointment I caused him to feel.

Ten years ago, my life was the kind of headline people skim and then shake their heads at: drug addiction, crime, stints in prison. Back then, I was at war with myself and sabotaging everything good in my life.

Today, I'm proof that your past doesn't define your future.

For many years I looked for solutions in external things. All the booze, the drugs, the destruction of things and other people and myself, was to drown out the feelings that word came to represent. All the dark places I have been, the many mornings I woke up with teeth missing or a cracked jaw, a torn gullet or a knife wound, or hooked up to an ECG for alcohol and cocaine abuse. The prison sentences for hurting people. The hours I spent in a cell, not remembering the night before, certain that I'd gone too far and killed someone this time.

And throughout it all, that word was my black dot.

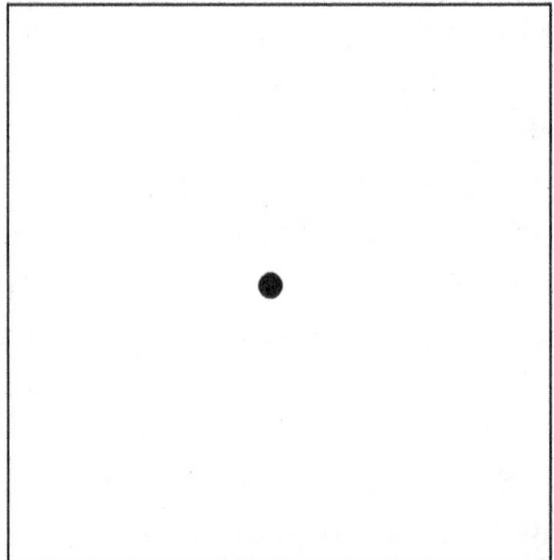

What do you see when you look at this image?

Most people say, 'A black dot.' They ignore the white space around it, even though the white space takes up almost the entire image.

That black dot is who we are. It represents our flaws, our trauma, our mistakes and our setbacks. You can't ignore the black dot. In fact, the picture only works because the dot is there. Without it, you've just got an empty frame.

The trick is to hold both truths at the same time: the dot is real, but it's a small part of a much bigger picture. The white space and the black dot only make sense because of each other. But most people stare at the dot. Obsess over it. They forget all the space that surrounds it, the space that's still available in which to create something new.

And that's where the real shift happens. I went in deep when I spoke about this in my TEDx Talk. The theme was 'Event Horizon' – which is, in Einstein's theory, the edge of a black hole. The point of no return. Once something crosses it, it's pulled into the unknown, never to escape. This is a feeling that a lot of people face with even some of life's smallest challenges.

For years, that's how I saw my past. Addiction. Prison. Trauma. Shame. I thought I'd crossed that line. I thought I was a lost cause, beyond the point of no return. It was dark, consuming, and anything positive felt out of reach. For me, it felt like there was no light at the end of the tunnel – and the black dot? That was the end.

But then I thought . . . what if it's the beginning?

Some people in astrophysics believe that a black hole might not be the end; it could be a portal to something entirely new. That's why I developed the theory I call 'Turning a Black Hole White' – the belief that our darkest moments hold the key to our evolution.

This black dot was a visual concept for one of the major turning points in my life, and one you will discover throughout this book. I stopped seeing the black hole as something to run from and started seeing it as something to lean into. Not a void. Not an ending. Just a small black dot on a huge white canvas.

We can't change our past. We can't change our childhood, our family, the things we didn't get. We can't undo the choices we made from a broken place. But we can choose how we see them. We can shine a light on those shadowy parts of ourselves. We can stop pretending they don't exist and stop letting them run the show. We can use them. Learn from them. *Grow through them.*

Every day is a new chance to step back from the dot and start using the rest of the page. The dot is still there. It always will be. But it doesn't define you. It's just the 'once upon a time'. And everything that really matters comes after.

We have, all of us, an infinite capacity to change the way we see ourselves, our life, and the endless opportunities that are waiting for us. If we truly want to.

Do you feel stuck? Like you should be doing something different, but you don't know what, never mind how? The first step in finding answers is to learn to ask the right questions. I once lifted my hand in a rehab group session and asked, 'What do you do if you know you have problems but don't know what they are?' This book is for people who want to learn to ask the right questions.

One of my revelations came when I was diagnosed with Anti-social Personality Disorder, Emotionally Unstable Personality Disorder, and Bipolar Type 2. A bundle of conditions that often earns its sufferers the famous but completely non-medical badge of 'psychopath'. When most people think of a psychopath, they picture a serial killer or an utterly cruel, remorseless person. But many people with these conditions lead full, loving lives.

My conditions mean that I can't feel certain emotions in the same way most other people can. I tend to think emotions rather than feel them. They also mean I don't really understand rules or anticipate consequences. And I am a terrible judge of risk, both to myself and to others. Now, for most people, being labelled a psychopath would not be a good thing. But for me it was transformative. It was the first step on a long road to make sense, eventually, of all the things I had never been able to do. It led me – after a lot of hard work – to a place where I was able to make peace with what I couldn't do, and instead focus on what I *could* do.

Because, after a life of believing I was beyond hope and utterly without value, it turned out there were some things I *was* good at.

If we were chatting today in my cosy café in Bali, or outside on the deck of my training centre in Tulum, Mexico, I'd start by telling you this: your history can be your greatest teacher, not your life sentence. The turning point came when I realized that my story – my pain, mistakes and failures – had value. When you see this value, and I mean truly see it, and the asset it can become in your life, you unlock a kind of power most people never tap into.

For example, I turned my knack for impulsive and addictive behaviour into a relentless drive for self-betterment and business success. The same qualities that once led me astray became the fuel I needed to create the life I have today.

Eleven years after I was in prison for the third time, I am a doctor of philosophy and the founder and CEO of The Coaching Masters, one of the world's largest and fastest-growing coaching academies in the world, a $25-million coaching academy that has trained over 13,000 people to become life coaches, and is growing, as of writing this book. It's the kind of success my old brain would have said was only for people who had won the lottery or been given some unfair advantage. It has turned out that every single thing I couldn't do is an important part of the story that I use to inspire coaches to use their own story to help others. My black dot transformed into a tiny pebble that was dropped into a pond, and the ripples just keep going outwards:

13,000 coaches transforming the lives of 50,000, 100,000, a million . . . And I have made it my life's work to help them deal with their own black dots. More pebbles dropping into more ponds, more ripples.

You probably haven't been labelled a psychopath, or been to the dark, extreme places I have been. But you will have faced adversity. It will have shaped who you are and how you approach life. You will have that voice in your head saying you aren't good enough. You will do things that are bad for you and struggle to make choices that benefit your life. You might find yourself scrolling through your phone, looking at the perfect lives that other people seem to be living, feeling stuck and hopeless and sad.

We all have our black dot. I want to show you how to turn it into a pebble dropped into a pond.

I can't promise it will be easy. But it is possible – and in this book, I will show you, practically, the things I have done to turn my life around. The proven techniques we use to teach our coaches, and which they then use across the world to unlock the potential of those they work with. Because here's the thing people don't realize with coaching training: you become your own first client. You dive into the tools, techniques and frameworks, and before you know it, you're applying them to your own life. You're forced to face yourself, your patterns, your habits and your stories. By the end, you're not the same person.

Coaching has been my lifeline. It's the thing that gives me purpose and the foundation for everything I've built and the person I am today.

But here's something the personal development industry probably doesn't want me to tell you, and it's certainly not something you'd expect a coach to say who has thought of writing a book to gather in some new coaching clients. But here it is: don't waste your money hiring a life coach. Hiring a coach is like being handed a fish – you'll get a meal, but then what? The real transformation happens when you become a fisherman.

This book is me showing you how to fish.

If you're looking for something real, something different, this is it. This is a no-nonsense guide to transformation: raw, straight-talking, and packed with actionable steps. By the time you're done, you'll have more than inspiration; you'll have the tools to create a life that's entirely your own, and step into a truly unlimited version of yourself.

Some parts of it may shock you, others may challenge you. I didn't want to write just another self-help book. I'm not a psychologist; I'm just a guy who made a whole lot of really bad decisions and was somehow able to turn his life around. But I have seen what happens when I tell my story, I've seen the spark of recognition in other people's eyes. I've heard them tell me how, though the details might be completely different, something about it feels like their life. I've seen, again and again, how the steps we take to be the best coaches we can be are the same steps we need to take to be the best versions of ourselves. And by 'best', I don't mean richest, or most successful; I mean fulfilled, as if you've finally arrived home in your own skin.

People often ask me if I regret the things I've done. And I always answer no. Not because I'm indifferent to the harm I have caused, but because I understand that every single experience, every mistake, every moment of darkness brought me to where I am today. And where I am today is a place of purpose, gratitude and action – something I wouldn't trade for anything. In this book, I want to be honest about my journey in all its extremity, and what I have learned at The Coaching Masters about what actually gets results, rather than the same old tired advice – self-help books that sugar-coat the hard stuff.

Some of my methods are controversial. All too often, I witness people preaching the same things that people want to hear, rather than what works and the things that are required to get real results.

We've got adversity all wrong. It's not just something to get through, it's the platform on which our success stories find their foundation. We all carry the echoes of old traumas, the scars from past mistakes, and the weight of unfulfilled dreams. These burdens become chains that tether us in place. But they don't have to. We can learn to stop letting our past define the limits of who we can be. We can take our adversity and transform it into the ultimate asset. If you have a dream, a passion, or even just a flicker of hope for change, listen up: you are not defined by your worst days. This is your framework for turning adversity into an asset and stepping into a life without limits.

So, if you're ready to take back control and create a life of value, let's get started.

This is your journey to becoming *unlimited.*

CHAPTER 1

A True Reflection

'You can't keep fucking doing this.'

I am stood, squinting at myself in the scratched, dull metal surface of a prison cell mirror. I am not allowed a glass mirror here, in case I use it to kill myself.

I am twenty-four, and the face looking back at me is one I have come to despise. Every bad thing I have done, there is that same face staring back at me. Every time I wake up, bruised, bloody, with teeth missing and fists scarred from knocking out other people's teeth, there it is, that face. I'm so sick of it. Violence has expanded until it has filled the hole at the centre of me.

It began with my dad, with the violence in his words, doled out to me and my mother. I would run back to my room and look in the mirror as I beat myself up. I'd punch myself in the temple as hard as I could, face red, veins popping, furious at myself for being a bad kid who deserved the things he said. There was a release in violence. I remember once, stealing the tiny diamond-tipped hammer from the emergency case on a bus and smashing every single bus shelter I walked past for two miles. And as the glass cascaded down in those neat little shards, I can remember it feeling so *right*. I was making the outside world match how I felt on the inside. I imagined the hundreds of people who would see that broken glass and wonder what had happened, and the answer was me. They would know that I had been there. That I existed.

At one point, when I was younger, I thought that becoming famous might be the solution. It could be a kind of mirror that I could use to show the world a different version of me. A good version. Perhaps one that my dad would be able to love. So, when I was seven, I studied singing and acting, and took dancing lessons. I didn't really care what I did. I just wanted to be famous. My parents were happy to support it. Up until that point, they hadn't really known what to do with me. Back in nursery, when it was 'visit your child day' and all the other kids were sitting quietly on the carpet, I was the odd one out, jumping up and banging a drum, singing happy birthday though it wasn't anyone's birthday. My impulsiveness was understood as naughtiness, as looking for attention. Maybe performing would be my thing?

I threw myself into it obsessively. I took every class, signed up for every show, practised for hours on end. Then, when I was eleven, I found myself at the house of an older male I had met through performing. What began as holding my hand became kissing and touching and then more. I froze, paralysed with confusion and fear.

At the time, I didn't even know what had happened. I just knew it must somehow be because I had done something to deserve it. Because I was bad. I stopped performing. It wasn't an escape any more. It was just another place I was bad. I started secondary school within weeks, and school became another battleground where I rebelled against authority, collecting red cards like badges of honour. I was disruptive and unruly to the point of school suggesting I get psychiatric help. A story told by my former teacher years later demonstrates the inward view I had of myself – she reminded me of a time when, after I was sent out of the class for my behaviour, while trying to console me she told me I was a good lad. My response was 'I'm not good, miss. I'm bad.'

All of the evidence agreed with me. By the age of fourteen, I had an Antisocial Behaviour Order (ASBO), and by fifteen, I was expelled from school, leaving with no qualifications under my belt. On the letter sent home it said, 'Lewis has been permanently expelled for refusing to accept the authority of staff.'

My dad was an alcoholic – and Mum, well, she wasn't far behind him. Drinking in our house was as normal as other families' Sunday roast. So drinking filled my time. And soon, it wasn't just the occasional drink. The way I saw it, it gave me the push I needed to be a bit bolder, a bit more reckless. Then came the weed – and the arrests started piling up too. My actions were really messing with my family, especially my little brother. I got him mixed up in my criminal lifestyle, having him do some of my dirty work. It was a messy phase of life – I'd disappear for days, then turn up at home looking like I'd been wrestling with bears. It wasn't a pretty sight.

They decided they needed to protect themselves. 'We're ring-fencing you from the family,' they said. 'You're hurting us, and it's got to stop.' The rejection just hammered home what I'd been thinking all along: I was bad and unlovable.

Instead of looking at myself and my behaviour, I just shrugged and went looking for love somewhere else. I met my first girlfriend at a party. Slid into her messages, and soon enough we were a thing. And it was like someone had turned a light on. I was finally feeling all those things I'd been yearning for – love, attention, significance. Her family was really nice too. Dinner invitations, TV sessions, the whole lot. It was this weird feeling of belonging I'd never felt with my own family. Being with her, it felt like I'd hit the jackpot. I became obsessed. I wanted to see her every day, and texted her all the time; it was like she was my world. For the first time, I was feeling good about myself, feeling loved and feeling normal.

But then the drinking started to get worse. And I noticed something else – I was getting more aggressive. One night, after downing a bottle of Jack Daniel's, I was at her place. We got into an argument; she told me she'd cheated on me. It felt like a bus had hit me. All those feelings of love and acceptance I'd been basking in vanished in an instant. I grabbed a big kitchen knife and slashed my neck. Of course I didn't deserve to be loved. I was bad. As the blood poured down my neck, I started fighting the paramedics. They had to pin me down, sedate me and stitch me up. The whole time, I was screaming, crying, begging them to let me die. I was beyond heartbroken; I was shattered.

After they'd taken me to the hospital to get patched up and I'd calmed down a bit, I did something insane. I yanked out the IV, stumbled out of the hospital in my bloody robe, and ran straight to her house. I can't even imagine how she must've felt when she saw me, covered in blood, looking like something out of a horror movie. I was speechless, just standing there. I was sectioned for one night, then let go. They chalked it up to heartbreak and booze and sent me on my way.

Not long after this, I found a car key on the pavement, and instead of handing it in like a normal person, I pocketed it. Stumbling upon the van it belonged to, I drunkenly decided that I now owned it. I drove that stolen van without a licence, chased by the police, through open fields. Even though I was only in second gear, I hit sixty miles per hour, the adrenaline pumping in my veins.

I didn't get far. My escape ended with me crashing into two parked cars. I tried to run but was tackled, and arrested for dangerous driving, vehicle theft, driving without a licence and possession of cannabis. I was given probation and community service, but I didn't feel like I had to bother with all that, so then I was sentenced to three months in a young offenders' institution. This was a world defined by power and violence. Inside those walls, I was shoulder to shoulder with teenagers sentenced for murder, and with gang members who wouldn't hesitate to knife you over five quid's worth of tobacco. Every inmate was trying to prove they were the toughest. Some of the tales would send shivers down your spine. Inmates throwing boiling water mixed with sugar onto each other. Lads bursting into cells wielding makeshift weapons like tuna cans or pool balls stuffed in socks, relentlessly beating their targets. As twisted as it sounds, I enjoyed parts of it. I was attracted to the danger, the recklessness.

Stepping out of prison for the first time, the taste of freedom was sweet. Once on the outside, I was hell-bent on making a name for myself. After all, the way I figured it, society had thrown its worst at me and I had thrived. Perhaps that's where I truly fit in, I thought. And yet, compared to the company I'd kept in jail, my crimes seemed almost petty. In prison, your introduction often starts with the weighty question 'What are you in for?' It's simple: the heftier the crime, the higher you're ranked. After being constantly bombarded with this hierarchy, my messed-up teenage brain adapted to it quickly, and I started looking forward to a return to jail, but with a more 'impressive' charge. Sounds crazy, I know. From my actions back then, you might've thought I was unshakable – a tough guy. But under that veneer, I was just a kid.

Everything shifted one night at a club when I was eighteen. Before I knew what was happening, my fist connected with some guy's face, and I didn't stop. I felt a surge of power. After that, feeling powerful became my new favourite thing. I didn't have an off switch. If I got into a fight with someone, my friends would have to drag me off them, snarling, or I would kill them. In that moment, they weren't a person, they were a problem with only one solution – violence. But more than that, I was finding the attention I had always craved. It might not have been the positive attention of a father saying 'well done'. But I felt a sense of pride in my crimes. In the extremity of my behaviour. It was my identity, my claim to significance.

When I was twenty, my dad was diagnosed with cancer. A big, chunky man, six feet tall, seventeen stone, he dwindled away before my eyes. Pancreatic cancer gripped him, diminishing him to a feeble, frail shell of the man I'd always feared. One day, I went to visit him in the hospital, and as I walked into the room, I saw him. Lifeless, his mouth agape, skin tinged yellow. They hadn't told us that he'd passed away the previous night. I boxed all that up and tried to ignore it. I redoubled my efforts to feel powerful.

I spiralled deeper into the abyss, taking cocaine four days in a row without eating or sleeping. I spent time in Magaluf and Ayia Napa, selling event tickets to tourists. I started dealing drugs, getting into conflict with major dealers, and even had run-ins with the Cypriot mafia. Those years are a blur of fights, more prison time, drugs, and multiple near-death experiences – including having my teeth knocked out, being slashed in the back with a knife, numerous overdoses and concussions, breaking my bones, and once even tearing my oesophagus and having surgical emphysema where the doctor told me there was a 50 per cent chance I would die.

Standing, looking in that scuffed mirror at the age of twenty-four, I was in prison because, one night, in a haze of vodka and cocaine, I'd found myself outside a train station. It was 4 a.m. and I'd jumped to the front of the taxi queue, flinging the door open to climb in. I turned around, and there he was – my dad. He was pointing and shouting in my face in his usual aggressive, demeaning way, tearing me down like he always did. What happened next is a blur. Maybe I blacked out. Maybe I saw red. Maybe I don't want to remember. But I do remember his voice cutting through me, making me feel utterly pathetic. I didn't hear the words, just the rage building inside me. It took over. I lifted my arm and swung as hard as I could. The next thing I saw was his face hitting the ground with a sickening thud that echoed in the night. Blood began to trickle slowly, dark and thick. Everything and everyone around me froze, the commotion silenced by the weight of what had just happened.

After what seemed like hours, the ambulance took him away, and the police put me in the car and took me to the station. I asked if he was dead, and they told me they couldn't tell me. The following morning, I woke up, not remembering what had happened. It wasn't unusual for me to wake up in a police cell with flashes of scenes from the night before, knowing that I had obviously done something really messed up but not quite being able to pinpoint what had happened and how bad it was going to be this time.

I started to piece the night together with the fragments of memory I had, and I was trying to figure out what was real and what wasn't. The police took me to an interview room and told me exactly what had happened. I had attacked a man called Vincent, and he was in a coma after suffering a brain haemorrhage. *Vincent?!* I thought to myself. My dad's name was Raymond. My head spun as I tried to fit this new information into my memories of the night before. I could vividly see my dad's face in that taxi queue, but as I started absorbing what the police were saying to me, I remembered that my dad had been dead for four years.

On the day I was sentenced, I found myself back in jail. This time it was eighteen months for grievous bodily harm. By then, I'd racked up eleven convictions and twenty-two offences.

I rang one of my mates to ask what people were saying. He

told me I was on the front page of the local paper, which wasn't exactly new. Then he said something that hit harder. One of my closest friends had posted a photograph of me outside the courthouse that day, and next to it one of me outside the same court-house seven years earlier. The caption read: 'Nothing Changes'.

People had said things like that before. But hearing it had come from him, someone I actually listened to, cut through the noise. He was right. Nothing had changed. I was right back where I'd started.

Sitting in my tiny cell, the smell of bleach and stale smoke hanging in the air, I tried to drown out the chaos of prison life, the shouting, the arguments, the tinny music blasting down the wing. But the loudest noise was in my own head. The truth was blunt and relentless: *It's you. It's you. It's you.* I couldn't blame anyone else any more. I was the problem.

That was the moment I looked at myself properly in the prison mirror. There was no dramatic breakthrough. Just a quiet, uncomfortable awareness that something had to change. I didn't know what that looked like, or how I'd do it. I only knew I couldn't keep repeating the same cycle.

I had spent years blaming everything and everyone around me for why my life was so tough. But where was that getting me? It was the same patterns again and again. Before I could start to change, I had to be honest about how I had got to where I was.

Blaming external factors goes hand in hand with seeking external solutions. I had been trying to find self-worth in violence, alcohol and drugs. But while those external solutions might have offered a temporary high, a fleeting sense of significance, they couldn't ever be the lasting solution because the problem wasn't external – it was inside me. They were like a plaster over a gaping wound. Real, lasting healing comes from a deep and genuine under-standing of ourselves. And the first step is taking responsibility.

This isn't easy. It's important to remember that taking responsibility doesn't mean you're to blame for what has happened to you. But if you're waiting for someone else to take responsibility for it, it's *your* life that is frozen. It's like being in quicksand – the more you struggle against the reality of your situation without taking responsibility, the deeper you sink. This only creates resentment. And resentment is toxic. It drains your energy, clouds your judgement and keeps you in a negative cycle. When you let resentment take hold of you, you're not just stuck; you're going backwards. And what's worse is that the people or circumstances you're resenting probably don't even know, or care, that you're holding on to all the frustration. They're out there living their lives, while you're the one stuck in a mental prison, clinging to a grudge that's doing nothing but hurting you. It's the biggest waste of energy there is.

Nelson Mandela, who had every reason to hold on to resentment after twenty-seven years in prison, understood that the only way to move forward and truly live is to let go of the anger and focus on what you can control – your actions, reactions and mindset. There is an incredible quote which is often attributed to him: 'Resentment is like drinking poison and then hoping it will kill your enemies.' It doesn't matter who you give your power to or what has happened in your life. Letting go of resentment isn't about being soft, gentle, weak or kind. It's about reclaiming your power. The moment you decide to shift your focus and energy onto the things you can influence, that's when everything changes. That's when real, lasting transformation begins.

I began to repeat a mantra in my head: *I don't deserve it but I will fix it.* Every time I began to spiral about how unfair my life had been: *I don't deserve it but I will fix it.* Every time I started to feel jealous of those people whose childhoods had been so much easier than mine: *I don't deserve it but I will fix it.* Because focusing on the past is focusing on the one thing you can't change. It can only result in frustration and anger as you remain more stuck than ever. If you focus on how the past has made you feel bad, you reinforce its power.

The Subconscious World

So often, the things that shape us are hard to see. The messages we have absorbed about who we are and the love, safety and happiness we deserve are invisible to us. They happen somewhere deep down in our brain – an invisible script whose lines we repeat again and again. My script was that I was worthless, incapable of deserving love, and I spent my young life trying to replace love with anything I could find. I chose the exact opposite of love. I chose destruction, violence and chemical oblivion because they felt like a kind of control. And once your pattern is set, you repeat it. Again and again and again. You look for what will make you happy again and again – in school, in friendships, in your romantic relationships and your job. Every time, you hear a little voice in your head saying 'you won't be good at that'. Every time, you don't think there's any point trying. It could be the reason you don't quit the job you hate and start your business. The reason you accept your romantic partner treating you badly, because the only alternative would be to be alone. The reason you can't eat right, or go to bed early or go to the gym. Of course, it doesn't help that advertisers spend billions crafting messages to exploit your feeling that something external will make you happy. That new pair of trainers, that perfect holiday, that new juicer, that final missing piece that will finally complete you. But you need to stop looking at external solutions. You need to start by looking honestly at yourself.

Our sense of ourselves is so often shaped in childhood. But you must remember that your parents were shaped by theirs. And their parents by theirs. And backwards for as many generations as there has been humanity. Everyone handing down their shit to the next generation, who hand it on to the next in turn. And so you need to stop blaming your parents. Yes, they almost certainly weren't perfect. But their parents definitely weren't, and neither were their parents before them. We will never get to the beginning of the chain. I wish I could go and give my grandad's grandad anger management classes, but I can't. You will never find the right person to blame.

Though the quote by the writer and abolitionist Frederick Douglass that 'it is easier to build strong children than repair broken adults' is certainly true, we have to work with what we've got. We can't change the past; we can only change things starting from now – this exact moment. Is it fair that you have to take the burden of all those generations on your shoulders and end the cycle now? Probably not. But to flip the quote made famous by Spider-Man: with great responsibility comes great power. Because if you look at it from another angle, what an opportunity you now have – the power to put down that heavy burden and walk forward without it into the future. To stop blaming the past and create a new future. Because *you don't deserve it, but you will fix it.*

It won't be easy. We can twist pretty much anything to fit our script. These stories keep us stuck. They limit us. That's why when you go into the pub you see the same guys sitting up at the bar, or you'll hear your friend still moaning about their job or partner, even though they have been saying the same thing for the last ten years. Think about your daily routine. You wake up, maybe grab the same coffee, take the same route to work, and even eat the same lunch. You think you're choosing these things, but are you really? Could it just be your brain on auto-pilot, following patterns you've been building for years? Even the big decisions, like a career choice or how you react in an argument, have all been shaped by previous experiences and conditioning that have quietly moulded your responses. If you feel stuck, there's a good chance it's your script keeping you stuck. Because, like a familiar, comforting bedtime story when you're a child, the stories we tell ourselves become comforting, even though they're bad for us.

You can see this in a really simple way. Have you ever noticed how easy it is to sort out someone else's life but how hard it is to fix your own? When your friend is telling you about their latest romantic disaster, or their toxic boss, the solution feels so obvious. But when the same sort of problem is happening to you, it's more complicated than they understand. This is exactly the same for everyone. Our stories are like a piece of material pulled across a mirror, making everything we see blurry. For most of us, all we have is a feeling that something isn't quite right. That there's something holding us back that we can't quite put our finger on. It's not there in that part of our mind that we're aware of, where we make decisions. It's somewhere deeper, underneath all that.

I remember I was sitting around the dinner table with an ex-girlfriend of mine and her parents once. She would often refuse to try new foods, but on this occasion, she mentioned a food she was thinking of trying. Her mum immediately responded, 'Oh no, you wouldn't like that.' And she nodded along. I didn't think much of it at the time. But these days, it feels like a perfect example of how these stories get created and transmitted. Who knows where that particular story started – perhaps my ex had genuinely been a fussy eater at some point. Or perhaps her mum had been a fussy eater, and was nervous of cooking her child new foods. However it started, once my ex-girlfriend became the sort of person who didn't try new foods, that was it. Not only did she not know all the foods she might have loved because she never tried them, she was so unused to different flavours and textures that she really might not have actually liked them, even if she did try them, because our stories end up shaping our reality.

Mental Smokescreens

The problem is your brain doesn't want you to see the truth. Your brain's job is to keep you alive. Sometimes that goal aligns with you feeling good. It's why falling in love feels good and eating sugar tastes good and holding a hot pan feels bad. But it gets more complicated when your brain has to decide between things that feel good in the short term but might not be the best thing for you long-term. Solving that next level on your mobile game might make you feel good in the short term, but you should actually be writing that report for work. Staying in your nice warm bed feels better than getting up. Running one mile feels better than running three. And the stories that you have told yourself are so deep, so familiar and so comforting that it feels bad to try to step away from them. It's like if you hurt your arm, you hold it close to you and try to stop anyone from examining it because it will hurt. Our stories often begin in response to a *mental* wound of some sort. Mine began in response to the behaviour of my father. But they don't have to be this big and dramatic. Any time that you have felt stress, trauma, grief or betrayal, you can be wounded.

At the moment, you are almost certainly in one of two camps: you either know you have mental wounds and you want to know why they're causing you to act in the way that you do – or you don't think you have any wounds. This second camp is by far the hardest because it means that your subconscious mind has patched your wounds up and stepped in as a 'protector', creating beliefs and defence mechanisms that seemingly keep you 'safe'. The problem is that, while those defences may have kept you safe in that moment, they almost certainly aren't how you should be living your life.

To take one example, it used to be a very common child-rearing technique to let a young baby 'cry it out'. This meant that when they cried, you shouldn't go and comfort them, but let them soothe themselves. It was thought that this was an essential skill that all people should learn how to do – to soothe yourself. These days, that technique, though it still has its believers, has masses of detractors. Because it turns out that when we cry and no one comes to us, what we learn is that no one cares when we cry. But instead of that producing some magic inner well of self-sufficiency, what that means for a lot of people is that they spend their whole life repeating that pattern of crying for help but never receiving it. Or, worse, they never connect with people, because what's the point – no one ever comes when you need them anyway.

So, you spend your life engaging in behaviours that make sense for a child crying in a cot, but when applied in adult life just lead to unhappiness. The problem is that the unhappiness feels like home. The romantic partner who treats you meanly feels like home. The expectation that what you want doesn't matter feels like home. The good, kind, decent caring person who might actually give you what you want doesn't feel like home. They might feel dull, or too keen. That job that doesn't care who you are and makes you feel unfulfilled and unseen? That feels like home. The thought of making a change to something you care about? That doesn't feel like home. That feels scary.

So, we create entire stories to avoid feeling bad.

The Danger of Denial

It's an oldie but a goodie that denial is a river we all swim in. A classic example with me was alcohol and drugs. Even when I was by anyone's definition clearly an addict, if you'd asked me, I would have told you it was a choice. I liked drink and I liked drugs; I liked the way they made me feel. The fact I couldn't go for a couple of hours without shaking and needing a hit of something? The idea that the thought of stopping filled me with utter dread? Nah, I'm fine. I'm in control. I'm a legend.

Denial is our brain's way of saying, 'Nope, that's too much for me right now!' It blocks out uncomfortable realities or truths, helping us to avoid pain or anxiety in the moment. But while denial can feel like a cosy hiding spot, it stops you from processing and addressing what's really going on. It's like hitting snooze on an alarm, but you can only avoid waking up for so long. The bigger problem is that if you don't know what your issues are, you can never resolve them.

The first step is to talk about how you really feel. At the heart of counselling, therapy, psychotherapy, psychiatry, coaching and mentoring lies one fundamental practice – talking. Most of the time, in day-to-day life, we barely scratch the surface when talking to other people. Can you imagine how someone would react if they asked how you were and you said something other than 'All good thanks, how are you?' We talk endlessly about TV shows, holiday plans or the weather, but who's diving into the deep waters of how we're actually feeling?

We need to start by mapping the edges of our own wounds, our stories and our denial. We need to shine a light on these shadowy places. Because we can't change something we can't see. Every Alcoholics Anonymous and Narcotics Anonymous meeting begins with everyone standing up, saying their name and declaring they're an addict. You might not be an addict, but that process of actively naming and admitting what you want to fix – that is the key first step.

Your Reality Check Journal

A good first step is to start a Reality Check Journal. Every evening, write down one thing you might be ignoring or brushing off from your day. A good way to spot denial is by listening to phrases like 'It's fine' or 'It's not a big deal'. Ask yourself: *What's the truth here? What am I avoiding?* You don't have to solve it – just name it. Naming it is step one. At the same time, note down larger things about yourself that occur. Are you quiet or loud? Are you intense or laid-back? Are you funny or serious? Can you keep a secret or not? Are you confident or shy?

If you're feeling brave enough, you can also ask close friends and family; they'll usually notice qualities and behaviours in you that you don't notice yourself. Remember not to get defensive. If you are tempted to justify, explain or excuse, that's a classic sign of denial. Remind yourself that your friends and family are simply trying to give you the truth that you've asked for, however uncomfortable that must be. But take special notice of the things that provoke the strongest reaction in you, because they may well be your triggers.

Controlling Triggers

Triggers are those annoying landmines that set us off, often without us even realizing why. One minute, you're fine; the next, you're snapping at someone or spiralling into old patterns. Why? Because triggers mess with your subconscious, activating beliefs and memories you've probably buried so deep you forgot they were even there. When something around you feels like a flashback to a past experience, especially one loaded with emotion, your brain reacts like it's happening all over again, even if the current situation doesn't really call for it. Back in the caveman days, that fight-or-flight response was a lifesaver when a sabre-toothed tiger appeared. The amygdala, the part of your brain that handles emotional processing, kicks into high gear during a perceived threat, hijacking your rational thinking to get you out of danger. But today, the 'threats' are usually things like a tough email, a snarky comment or something not going your way – not exactly life-and-death stuff. The problem is your brain doesn't know the difference. So it reacts as if your life is on the line, which is why your response to triggers can sometimes feel completely over the top.

To take control, alongside your Reality Check Journal, try creating a Trigger Map. Over a week, write down every moment you feel triggered, noting what happened and how you reacted. Be specific – was it your boss's condescending tone, the smell of their aftershave, or something else? At the end of the week, look for patterns and ask yourself what deeper belief or memory might be tied to each trigger. For example, maybe that tone from your boss reminded you of being criticized as a kid. Don't worry about solutions yet.

Rationalizations

Also pay special attention to the moments when you feel yourself desperate to justify or explain something. Rationalization is like putting a pretty bow on something that's actually a mess. You create logical-sounding excuses to avoid uncomfortable truths. For example, you might say, 'I didn't really want that promotion anyway,' when deep down, you're gutted. It might feel convincing in the moment, but it keeps you from seeing the truth.

When you catch yourself justifying something, ask yourself: *Why do I believe that? Why does that matter? What's really underneath this thought?* This helps to peel back the layers, making it harder to hide behind excuses. When we avoid dealing with bad feelings by creating a rationalization of why they're not bad at all, they don't go away, they're just repressed and fester in the darkness. Repression is like sweeping broken glass under a rug. Your mind shoves painful thoughts or memories away. It's a survival mechanism, protecting you from overwhelm. But it's still there and, over time, it overflows, spilling into your mood, health and relationships without you realizing it.

Find Your Safe Space

Here's a simple exercise to uncover what's hiding under the surface. Find a quiet spot, close your eyes, and breathe until you feel calm. Then, picture a safe space in your mind – somewhere that feels comforting, like a beach, a forest or a cosy room. Focus on the details: the sounds, smells and textures that make it feel secure. Once you're relaxed, gently ask yourself: *Is there something I need to see or remember right now? What memory or feeling am I ready to explore?* Sit with whatever comes up – whether it's a faint image, a word, or just a vague feeling. Let it flow without overthinking or judgement. When you're ready, open your eyes and jot down anything that comes to mind. It might make sense immediately or take some time to connect the dots. Repression thrives on being ignored, so this exercise gives it space to come into the light. No force. No pressure. You're not here to fix anything yet; you're simply inviting awareness. If something heavy comes up and feels too much to handle, consider seeking professional support to explore it further, as sometimes repressed memories can be painful and hard to process alone.

Also start to pay attention to the other people that cause you to feel bad. Note down what qualities they have. Do you notice any patterns? Do you feel as if multiple people you know all behave in the same way? There is a good chance that you might be projecting aspects of yourself onto them. Projection is like holding up a mirror to someone else but refusing to look at your own reflection. It's when you take qualities or feelings you dislike in yourself and pin them on another person. For example, accusing someone of being controlling when, in reality, you fear losing control yourself. Or perhaps you feel like they are selfish because you have always had to look after yourself.

The Mirror Test

The next time someone irritates or triggers you, try the Mirror Test. Pause and ask yourself: *What about this person's behaviour feels familiar? Have I ever done something similar?* This isn't about excusing their actions, but about spotting where your reaction to them might be rooted in your own stuff. Growth starts when the finger-pointing stops. Once you realize it's more about you than it is about them, you get the power back. You can work on yourself, and suddenly the person that once irritated you doesn't any more – because all that was really irritating you was the subconscious trigger that deep down you knew you didn't like something about yourself.

Displacement is similar to projection, but for things that happen outside your control. It redirects emotions from a 'dangerous' object to a 'safer' one. For example, someone might displace their anger towards their boss by taking it out on their family, which fails to address the root cause of the anger. You won't be aware you're practising displacement; it's another sneaky way of your brain controlling your thoughts in a seemingly safer way.

Once you're tracking all of the various ways that you act, your triggers, your rationalizations and projections, the next stage is pulling it all together and thinking about whether you can change your responses. Once you've connected the dots, you might decide how to respond next time. Write it out: 'When my boss uses that tone, I'll take a breath and remind myself it's not personal.' When a trigger creeps in, pause and visualize your response before acting. It's not about getting it perfect every time, but about gradually shifting from reacting on autopilot to consciously responding.

The Pause-and-Redirect Method

When you notice yourself snapping or feeling irritable, take a deep breath and ask yourself: *Who or what am I really upset with? What am I avoiding by taking it out in this way?* Then, redirect that emotion into a physical outlet – go for a walk, punch a pillow, or write an angry letter (and burn it). This gives the emotion somewhere to go without hurting someone else. Just because you have a thought, it doesn't mean you *are* that thought. It's just a passing cloud in your mindscape. Thoughts come and go. Some are good, some are bad. But it's vital to remember that they're not the full story of who we are. They're fleeting moments in our brains, not concrete definitions of our identity.

Visualize your thoughts as cars on a motorway. You can notice them, and watch them zip by, but you don't have to jump in for a ride every single time. Or imagine they're like stations on an old radio. Sometimes you need to fiddle around with the dial to get a clearer signal, or even change the station completely.

This is all part of the process of getting a true reflection of yourself. It might feel strange and unnatural at first. It might feel embarrassing to be making this effort and spending this much time on looking at yourself. You might have a voice in your head telling you that it's self-indulgent and embarrassing, or cringe. That other people don't need to do this stuff, so why are you doing it? This goes double if you're a man who has been taught that you should be strong and silent, self-contained and self-sufficient, with a stiff upper lip. But that feeling is the ultimate act of denial. That is the part of your script that says you are not worth the effort. That you don't deserve care.

But you must ignore that voice. Because you *are* worth it. You deserve to take care of yourself. You deserve maximum effort. There is nothing more important than you working out what is going on beneath your conscious thoughts. Because it shapes everything else. The patterns of our actions. The places and people where we go looking for love. Our entire outlook on what we are capable of is built on these foundations. Before we can turn adversity into an asset, we must accept that we have faced it. Then we can explore how we transform it.

Key Takeaways

- Take ownership of your life. Blaming external factors is a waste of time and energy.
- The reason you are where you are is you. That isn't a problem. That's the solution.
- Look your adversity in the eye. Before you can do anything else, you need to be honest about what you have faced.
- Denial, excuses and mental smokescreens may feel protective, but they're traps.
- Awareness shines a light on those automatic defences, exposing what's been holding you back.
- Sketch your subconscious. You need to start to identify the shape of the stories your brain has told you to keep you safe.
- Connect thought to action. Learn to recognize your triggers, rationalizations and displacements. These are what form the patterns that have got you to where you are.

In the following chapters we'll look at ways we can unpick those old stories and write new ones. We'll look at how to live with bravery and authenticity, through purpose-driven action. We'll look at how to face the things that scare us, and even learn to like discomfort. We'll examine how we form the habits that harm us, and how we can learn to hack our brains to develop habits that help us. We'll also learn the most difficult thing of all – how to come back from the hardest of knock-backs, to reframe weaknesses as strengths and failures as the path to success. We'll concentrate on our actions and how we actually deliver change.

But you can't skip this first stage. Like a boxer doing cardio training as hard as they can, so that they still have energy in the twelfth round, you need to put the preparation in now.

Everything else that will follow in this book is built on the idea of looking in a mirror and seeing your true reflection – just as in that scratched, dull metal surface in a prison cell, for the first time, I saw mine.

CHAPTER 2

Rewrite Your Reality

**'And what about the trainers of that one in the blue tracksuit?
Where do you even buy trainers that shit?!'**

I am stood outside a drug and alcohol rehabilitation centre in
Portsmouth with one of the other residents and, as usual, I am
picking apart everyone else in our session. Their age, their looks,
the drugs they took, what they're wearing, looking for ways that
I am different to them.

Since that day a year before when I had stood in front of
my cell mirror and felt that incredible surge of energy where I
realized I needed to change, I had made undeniable progress.
The way I have always described it is that it felt like, for the first
time, my life began to spiral into control. You might not have
heard that saying before, though I bet you've heard of its ugly
reflection – spiralling *out* of control. Suddenly it felt as if I was
walking the right way on the airport conveyor belt. I had taken
the first step and acknowledged that I was the problem *and* the
solution. I then established a routine, immersing myself in books
and hitting the gym. I signed up for maths and English in the
education department and enrolled in the Rehabilitation for
Addictive Prisoners Trust (RAPT) programme. My plate was
full, yet my progress seemed microscopic. I wasn't just starting
from square one, but at a daunting minus ten. In the education
department, defiantly, I would fold my arms across my chest,

my ego barely disguising the fear of failure. Emotionally, I was stunted, a toddler in the body of a man.

Planting Belief

A turning point came when Suzie, one of the prison tutors, sat beside me during a maths lesson and asked me a simple question – 'What's the matter?' It was as if no one had genuinely considered my feelings before. All my pent-up confusion and frustration tumbled out at that moment as I said, 'I don't understand.' What confused me more was that I had said that, having not even attempted to understand what was being taught. Confused by my own words, I reflected and realized that I was scared that my dad's opinion of me as stupid was keeping me from even attempting to understand. It felt safer to retreat behind defiance than to risk exposing myself as the buffoon I thought I was. Yet Suzie was patient and supportive, guiding me through basic calculations on a par with a ten-year-old's level. With Suzie's support, I started to learn – and learn fast.

One day, I asked Suzie for a challenge to test myself. She taught me pi, which I picked up quickly. I then went back to my cell, and the next day I told her I had memorized pi to 100 decimal places. She laughed it off, but when I recited it at around five numbers a second, she was amazed; I then returned to my cell and learned it to 500 decimal places. I was shocked – how was I able to do this? I can tell you . . . belief. Suzie had sparked something in me that allowed me to try, and through my progress I was becoming empowered. I felt a new sense of significance, but it was coming from a strange place: it was coming from inside. I was proud of myself.

At one point, I asked Suzie a question that popped into my

head: 'Suzie, do you think I could ever make it to university?' I will never forget the unshakable certainty that flashed across her face as she met my gaze and, without hesitation, said, 'Of course you can.' I had never entertained the idea of university. I had been expelled from school a decade before at fifteen years old, leaving with no qualifications whatsoever. I had assumed it was reserved for smart kids, not someone like me. And yet, with just a few words from Suzie, I suddenly believed it was possible.

That level of faith she had in me . . . it felt alien, yet inspiring. Her belief planted a seed within me, a glimmer of self-confidence I'd never had. It's strange how hearing someone else believe in your potential can ignite a spark within you. That spark then fuelled a goal for me – get to university and sit alongside the 'smart kids', and prove my worth to everyone.

I kept going to the RAPT sessions too, even if it was some-times hard to see how they were useful. A roomful of hardened inmates, trying to articulate how they felt. We'd sit in a circle and the facilitators would ask us how we were feeling, really looking us in the eye. Nine out of ten inmates would reply, 'Alright.' The odd person might say, 'Hungry.' Then everyone would smirk. So much of prison life was about projecting this attitude of tough-ness. You didn't want people thinking they could mess with you. So, of course, everyone kept that front up. However, those work-shops did give me a vocabulary to understand and express my emotions better.

Then, one day, a guest speaker told us about a scheme on the south coast that we could apply for. It was £20,000, paid for by the government. They only selected a small proportion of the people who applied. I was pretty sure I was nowhere near as serious a case as loads of other people, so was pretty sure I wouldn't get in. But then I got the letter that I was successful.

I was picked up from the prison gates and driven straight

to the rehab centre, clutching my care plan – a cold, clinical summary of my life. Alcohol dependency, narcotics dependency, anger issues, grief, dual diagnosis, attachment issues, childhood emotional neglect, physical and emotional abuse, rejection, self-neglect. But rather than acting like a wake-up call, seeing this list made me more resistant. Of course my life was a mess. What did they expect? How could it ever have been anything else? The deck felt so stacked against me, and I was playing a game I didn't know how to win.

I still wanted to change. I had to. But I didn't know how. I had to start doing things differently, but I was still so resistant to anything new that was put in front of me. I had a hard shell around me. I couldn't believe that any of these people really cared about me. My own family didn't, so why should they? *You're just here for the money*, I spat at them. I didn't trust them as far as I could throw them. I kept myself to myself and did the bare minimum, but was counting the days until I could get out of there. I had convinced myself that these people were nothing like me. They were fuckups. I might not have been in a prison cell any more, but looking back I realize I was trapped in something even harder to get out of – my mindset.

But that day, when I started going in on that guy's trainers, the other resident waited for me to finish. Then he took a final drag on his cigarette. 'Why don't you stop looking for ways we're different to you.' He stamped the butt out and put it in his top pocket. 'And start looking for all the ways we're the same.' Then he turned round and went back inside.

I don't know why, but something in me shifted. Maybe it was the way he said it with such quiet force. Not angry, but as if he was tired of listening to my shit, like he was sad for me. Maybe it was just the right words at the right time. Whatever it was, I went back inside and that session I listened – I properly listened to what they were saying. I listened to their pain, to their descriptions of their relationships with their families. I listened to how they felt and realized just how similar to me it all was. When it was my turn to speak, I started trying to be as honest as they were. It wasn't easy at first; I was so used to keeping everyone at arm's length. But day by day, session by session, I began opening up more, chatting, and asking questions. And to my surprise, people did care. They listened, and they sympathized. And I realized how important it is to feel like you are listened to. That you are seen. I became so good at talking that a simple 'How are you?' would unleash a waterfall of words and emotional confessions. But it wasn't all straightforward progress.

My brain is a tricky bastard, and it loves to mess with me. One time, I decided the counsellors were all just trying to brainwash me. I sat, arms crossed, convinced of their plot. During a group therapy session, I decided to tell them what I thought of them. 'I know what you're doing, you're trying to brainwash me!' One counsellor called me out. She watched my grin turn into a look of complete embarrassment as her words hit me like a slap to the face: 'Lewis, your best thinking has landed you in prison and now into rehab. Maybe your brain needs a good wash.' I realized she was absolutely right. My way of thinking had been a total dead end, causing havoc and landing me back in prison again and again. I was a hamster stuck in a wheel, repeating the same mistakes. I decided to give their methods a shot.

The Real-You Note

I dived into the typical self-help stuff. It was gruelling and uncomfortable, but I did it. The affirmations, the journaling, the gratitude lists, the opening up in therapy sessions – it all became part of my daily routine. Even when I stumbled, even when I doubted, I stuck with it. Because my way? It wasn't working. Sometimes the hardest thing to do is to admit that you can't do it alone, and that you need to try someone else's way.

Of course, it wasn't sunshine and rainbows. Every day I'd be in a mental tug of war, trying to convince myself that actually I could tackle all this alone. 'I'm not like these lot,' I'd mutter to myself. And I won't lie; there were moments when doing harm to myself seemed like the only way to silence the chaos in my head.

Then, one evening, after I'd survived another day in rehab – and, most importantly, stayed clean and sober – it felt like a victory. That's when I decided to jot down a note, a reminder for the 'future me' for those dark days when it feels like there's no end in sight.

Dear Lewis. You've felt like this before. You're going to feel like this again. It will pass. You're doing the right thing. Keep going.

Love, the real Lewis.

I needed to see it in black and white, to remind myself of the man I could be. I slapped that note on the wall, and every time those doubts would start creeping in, I'd read it. I'd remind myself that feelings are like the British weather, constantly changing, and making a lifelong decision based on a passing storm was a bad idea.

A mantra I picked up in rehab sums it up: 'This too shall pass.' Each time I'd have a right old scrap with myself, threatening to ruin all the progress I'd made, I'd take a look at the note – and after I had managed to ride out the storm and see a glimmer of sunlight after the rain, I'd scribble my signature on the note. Before I knew it, that note was a roadmap of my victories. And then, one day, I realized I didn't need to look at the note any more.

This was my first real win in wrangling my thoughts. And the awareness that I had the power to do that? It was a total game-changer. If I could change my thoughts, I could change my life.

It might sound simple, but here's the truth: you *can* change your mind. Everything we've talked about so far – all the shit that's shaped you, all the beliefs that sit under the surface like rot beneath floorboards – that stuff can be dug up and rebuilt piece by piece.

A Demolition Site

Most people treat their mind like a storage unit, crammed full of old boxes stacked from floor to ceiling in messy piles. Childhood traumas. Outdated rules. Other people's opinions. Shame. Guilt. Fear. It's dusty, it's dark, and half the stuff in there isn't even yours. But you keep it anyway. Because going in there and moving stuff about feels too big a job. Letting go of it feels dangerous. So you just keep the door closed.

And then someone like me walks in and says, 'Let's throw out that belief', or 'What if that story you've been telling yourself is total bullshit?' Let's get rid of these old dusty boxes and get some light in here, see what we're working with. And your gut reaction? Slam the door shut. Lock it. Say, 'No space in here, mate.'

But your mind isn't a storage unit. It's a demolition site. You weren't born with limits; you learned them. And if you learned them, you can *unlearn* them. But first, you've got to get messy. You've got to tear down some walls. Rip out the bad wiring.

Smash the stuff that no longer serves you, even if it's been there for decades. You might get some dust in your hair, but only then can you start building back something stronger. Not perfect. Not pretty. But *real*.

The Elastic Mind

You may have heard of the idea of a fixed or a growth mindset. The concept was coined by the psychologist Carol Dweck, as part of her work exploring how a person's beliefs about their own capabilities impact their lives, as set out in her book *Mindset: The New Psychology of Success*.

For our purposes here, it's useful to think about a few key ways this idea plays out. Those people with a fixed mindset believe that their abilities and intelligence are fixed and cannot change. Whereas someone with a growth mindset believes that these things can be developed with effort. A fixed mindset will avoid challenges in case they can't do something, whereas a growth mindset sees challenges as an opportunity to get better. A fixed mindset sees effort as pointless. A growth mindset sees it as essential. A fixed mindset finds it difficult to receive feedback or criticism and will become demotivated. A growth mindset sees it as essential to getting better at something. A fixed mindset feels threatened by the success of others. A growth mindset is inspired and wants to learn more from the success of others. A fixed mindset gives up at the first bump in the road. A growth mindset has resilience and uses setbacks as an opportunity to learn.

The first thing to realize is that most people are a blend of both, and the balance can change in different situations. As with all of the different aspects of ourselves we covered in the first chapter, our ability to keep a growth mindset will come down to a range of subconscious factors. You may have one colleague whose feedback is like nails down a chalkboard whatever they say. You might be able to pour your full effort into some parts of your life but switch off totally in others. As ever, it's often easier to see these things in other people than ourselves. But try to be totally honest with yourself as you think about your mindset in different parts of your life. Think about the last time you faced a challenge. How did you react? The last time you got a piece of feedback. How did it feel? Did someone you know get a promotion or succeed in their professional life? What was your honest response? It doesn't matter if you are uncovering some painful realizations right now – even if you do end up diagnosing yourself with a fixed mindset, the key thing to focus on is that your mindset can change. Whatever it is currently, if you want to, you can change your mindset.

After the honest assessment of yourself in Chapter 1, this is the biggest foundational principle in this whole book. Because it is absolutely essential to turning your adversity into an asset. Once you learn how to move into a growth mindset, adversity stops becoming something to fear. It is no longer something to avoid; you won't feel sorry for yourself when you experience it. Instead, it becomes the platform you build your success upon.

I have been lucky enough to meet some remarkable people as part of my *Adversities to Assets* podcast. There's Toby Gutteridge, a former Royal Marine whose life was changed for ever when a Taliban bullet shattered his spinal cord. Paralysed from the neck down and declared dead by his comrades, he defied every odd and clawed his way back – and founded the Bravery extreme sports brand, which does incredible charity work. And Alex Lewis, who suffered a devastating illness that led to the amputation of his arms and legs. He was able to take this incredible adversity and become the first quadruple amputee to kayak around the southern tip of Greenland. And Pam Warren, who was in a catastrophic train crash that left her with severe burns. But surviving wasn't enough for Pam – she wanted to make a difference. She became a fierce advocate for train safety and a voice for burn survivors everywhere. Almost without exception, they and the other remarkable people I have spoken to were able to face the very biggest of setbacks because they had the mindset that allowed them to.

Some of you may be rolling your eyes at this and saying it's not that easy. You're absolutely right, it's not. But it is *possible*. It's something you will have to spend your life working on. You can't just hit a switch and that's it from that day on. Just like you can't go to the gym, work out your muscles once, and that's it. You're going to have to commit to exercising your growth mindset regularly. You have a miraculous three pounds of soft grey-pink matter in your skull made up of 100 billion neurons and 300 trillion connections. And it has an almost infinite capacity to reorganize itself. Every time you learn something new – a new skill, a different way of thinking, or even just how to use a new app – your brain is rewiring itself.

The more you practise something, the stronger those connections become, turning what was once difficult into second nature. The scientific name for this process is neuroplasticity (which the brain invented, along with the name for everything in the universe). But neuroplasticity isn't just about learning new stuff; it's also your brain's way of healing and bouncing back from setbacks. For instance, when someone suffers a brain injury, neuroplasticity allows the brain to find new ways to compensate for lost functions. Stroke survivors often relearn how to move or speak again because their brains create new pathways to bypass the damaged areas. Now, think about what this means for you.

If your brain can adapt and grow after something as serious as a stroke, imagine what it can do with a healthy, albeit maybe partially 'fixed mindset', brain. Whether it's mastering a new skill or changing a long-held belief, your brain is up for the challenge. It's not stuck – it's a living, evolving part of you, ready to transform as long as you're willing to do the work.

When I first read the book *The Power of Your Subconscious Mind* by Dr Joseph Murphy, I was blown away. Some of the things described can only be considered miracles. People curing their chronic illnesses and using their brains to discover trauma that had manifested into physical symptoms. Dr Murphy talks about how our thoughts and beliefs, deeply rooted in our subconscious, can manifest in our physical bodies. The most powerful story in the book, documented by hospital records, is about a girl named Emily who had serious chronic sinus problems. Despite multiple surgeries, her condition wouldn't go away. It wasn't until she went into therapy that she began to see the deeper psychological roots of her condition, and discovered that her sinus issues were a subconscious way of relating to her father, who had suffered from the same issue. This was the true origin of her problem. This emotional connection and unresolved trauma had been influencing her physical health. By understanding this link, she was able to address the emotional root of her condition. Once she processed these emotional wounds, her physical symptoms began to improve, and she no longer required further medical treatment.

This might sound a bit out there, but you will probably have heard of the placebo effect. This is the response in which a significant proportion of patients experience real improvements in their symptoms after receiving a treatment that has no active ingredient. It's so powerful that scientists have to build a process into every drug trial to try to account for it. And if you think about it, it totally makes sense. Everything we feel or experience is filtered through our brains. Have you ever had the experience where a dressing gown across a chair looks like someone hiding in your bedroom, and for a moment your body reacts as if it is? Your system is flooded with adrenaline. You jump out of bed and switch the light on, your heart pounding. It's just a dressing gown on the chair. But your misperception shaped your physical reality massively.

And here's the dark side. Just as positive beliefs can heal, negative ones can destroy. Chronic stress, anxiety, and relentless negative self-talk can manifest as physical problems – things like high blood pressure, heart disease and a weakened immune system. Your mind, in all its complexity, absorbs what you feed it. Tell it you're doomed, and it might start paving the way to your downfall. Ever heard of the 'nocebo effect'? It's the twisted twin of the placebo effect – where negative expectations lead to negative outcomes. Some people, given a terminal diagnosis, die almost exactly when predicted, not because the prognosis was spot on but because their subconscious accepted that timeline as fact. That's how powerful your mind can be. Once you realize this, you can understand that your mind doesn't just shape your thoughts, it shapes your entire being.

Creating New Stories

Remember how I explained that every piece of information you've absorbed during your lifetime is processed in the part of your brain that you don't really have conscious access to, and is then used to form meaning, accepted as fact, which shapes your behaviours? Well, you can also feed it with new information. So far, we've talked about the conscious brain and the subconscious brain as separate and distinct. But, of course, they're connected. Part of what we were doing in Chapter 1 was some very simple ways of making subconscious things visible to our conscious brains. But, in reverse, we can also introduce new information using our conscious brain.

All you need to do is simply think good things about yourself, your abilities or your future. Better yet, you can say them out loud. The new information will be fed through to the subconscious, accepted as true and used to generate new, supportive, empowering stories and beliefs. These new stories and beliefs will allow you to make practical changes, reinforcing these new stories and beliefs. You will feel better about yourself. You will do better. Instead of a vicious spiral, you will find yourself in a virtuous circle.

With each small reaffirmation of your new stories, you will lay down a tiny bit more resilience to deal with the next setback. Have you ever felt in a place where you can't do anything? Where any task, however small, feels like too much? Maybe it's deciding which pizza to order. Or replying to a simple message from a friend. The thought of deciding literally anything just feels totally beyond you.

This is what happens when every single part of our mindset has been switched to fixed. Imagine a whole big board of lightbulbs on a set of circuits. As one of them turns red, so does another one and another, until the whole board is a cascade of red. But now imagine the reverse. Imagine a lightbulb instead turning green. Then another and another, until a whole wave of green sweeps across the control panel. You can turn some of those bulbs green right now.

You've made it this far in the book. That's not a small thing. I've asked you to do some tough things, I've told you some things that probably weren't easy to read. But you're here, you're reading these words. And you don't have to be. Some people will have stopped by now. But you haven't. Now take that win and think about what it might mean. Are you sometimes hard on yourself for giving up too quickly? Well, you haven't given up this time. Do you give yourself a rough ride for not reading enough? Well, you're reading now.

Find. Verbalize. Reverse

A very simple method we can apply is to find those negative, defensive, fixed mindset stories about ourselves, and just reverse them by verbalizing the direct opposite. If your head tells you that you're shy, nervous and socially awkward, then tell yourself you are a confident, charismatic, outgoing person. Don't worry if it feels silly at first. As we've discussed, your familiar old story has become comforting. Part of your brain's defence mechanism is to reject other stories that challenge it. The important thing is to say it. To bring the positive counter-story into being. But the more you state it, the more it will be accepted in your subconscious, and the more you'll start to accept and believe.

Another thing you can do is list your accomplishments, skills or qualities. This will almost certainly feel weird at first. We're really not used to being kind to ourselves like this, so your brain probably won't like it. At first, you might not be able to even think of enough for a list. Talk to someone you trust and ask them to suggest some positive things about you. One of the key early stages when I work with a coach is when I get them to tell their story to me. Then I tell it back to them as a list of positive accomplishments relating to their skills and qualities. Sometimes they try to resist – 'Oh, that's just normal, anyone would have done that.' But this is the whole point. You need to start telling your story in a different way.

Once you have your list, use 'I am' statements and connect them to power, so that it seeps into your identity. If you have overcome trauma, tell yourself, 'I am powerful because I am a survivor.' If you are balancing a busy family and professional life, tell yourself, 'I am powerful because I am capable.' If you have come out the other side of a difficult relationship, tell yourself, 'I am capable because I'm resilient and worthy of love.' It can be useful to focus on all of the things that often get overlooked. Do you look after other people in your life? Are you a caring friend, a generous aunt or uncle, a loyal partner? You might never articulate those things about yourself because they just are. Now is the time to speak them.

Identity isn't just a label we wear, it's the core of who we are. If you see yourself as someone who is constantly growing, adapting, and overcoming difficult things, that's exactly what you'll do. Your identity is who you are, and when you intentionally define it, you will start to see the things in your life that type of person would have. But your identity isn't a fixed thing. It is woven out of a thousand threads a day. And you can change the colour of those threads.

I have to admit, the first time I was introduced to this concept, I didn't know whether to laugh or cry. I had just arrived at rehab and I walked into a room called 'morning affirmations' at 9 a.m. I had no idea why I was surrounded by people singing what sounded to me like nursery rhymes. I listened a little closer and heard the words. 'I'm H-A-P-P-Y, I'm H-A-P-P-Y. I know I am, I'm sure I am, I'm H-A-P-P-Y.' They then stopped and, one by one, each would shout things to themselves. I thought they were mad. They'd shout things like, 'I'm a new person', 'I'm a strong person'. I reluctantly accepted the sheet of paper that was handed to me, which had a list of examples you could use, and gave it a go. When I walked out of that room for the first time, I had a strange feeling from within. I kid you not – after one session, I walked out feeling empowered. Needless to say, the effects of repeating this exercise every day for some months were powerful, to say the least.

These days, I look myself in the mirror and tell myself exactly who I want to be and what I'm going to achieve. I am absolutely certain that doing those affirmations for the first time was the key to changing my life, and if I hadn't forced myself to give it a try, I would still be sitting in prison, blaming every man and his dog for why I felt the way I did and why life was so unfair. You have everything you need right now to change your life, how you feel, and everything that comes with it. One of my favourite sayings is 'If you keep doing what you've always done, you'll keep getting what you've always got.' The flip side is if you do something different, you'll get something different. Take this option – because if nothing changes, nothing changes.

The Inner Coach and the Inner Critic

Another useful way of thinking about this is to imagine two voices we all have in our heads. We have the Inner Coach that tells us things like 'You're great', 'You can do this' and 'You deserve to be happy, fulfilled and successful'. It cheers us on and motivates us to go after what is important to us. We all also have the Inner Critic, which tells us things like 'You shouldn't even bother trying because you are going to fail anyway', 'Everyone will know you're an idiot' and 'You are not good enough, smart enough or pretty enough'. It encourages us to sabotage our progress and holds us back from achieving anything. Nobody is immune to the Inner Critic. No matter how successful you become, you will still have that voice that will tell you things like: 'You're about to mess this up', 'Why don't you just give up', 'You don't deserve this'. The difference between limited and unlimited people, is that unlimited people only allow their minds to be controlled by their Inner Coach rather than letting their Inner Critic spout irrational stories at them shaped by their past.

You may not hear two voices. Perhaps your Inner Coach and Inner Critic are singing together, like some perfectly harmonized melody. This will mean you don't know what thoughts you should bring to your attention and which thoughts you should let go of. The first thing you can do is separate the two voices. Ever find yourself in a mental tug of war, unsure if the thoughts swirling around in your head are helping you or just setting you up for failure? Not every voice in your head is on your side. Some are there to push you forward, while others are determined to hold you back. When you've got these duelling voices in your head, you can ask, *Who's really talking here?* Is it the real you, or is it just some self-sabotaging nonsense creeping in to mess with your head?

Borrow Your Inner Coach

If you can't tell, that's cool – there's another approach. Think about someone you admire, someone who's got their act together. Maybe it's a friend or family member who always seems to know the right thing to do. Or someone in the public eye who you especially admire. When you're too close to the problem, it helps to step back and borrow someone else's mindset. It's not about copying them; it's about using their perspective to realign yourself when you're feeling off-track. When your inner dialogue starts messing with you, and you can't trust your own gut, this is where you lean on that borrowed wisdom. It's like having a mental safety net until you can climb back up and take control again.

The reality is we all get lost in our heads sometimes. And when you're not where you need to be mentally, it's okay to lean on someone else's thoughts, decisions or even their confidence until you find your footing again. The key is to know when to tune out the noise and when to channel a different perspective – one that aligns with the direction you actually want to go. So, next time those conflicting voices start up in your head, don't just sit there and let them run the show. Step back, ask yourself what the real thing is that you would do, and if that doesn't cut it, channel the mindset of someone you respect. Ask yourself what they would do. Sometimes it's not about knowing exactly what to do – it's about knowing who to ask, even if that someone is a voice you've adopted until you're ready to trust your own again.

This Inner Critic I'm talking about is also commonly known as self-sabotage – a behaviour that kicks in when your actions clash with your beliefs. Take the scenario of career success. You're all in; you want a promotion, recognition and success. But deep down, your subconscious is still running the show, telling you that 'You're not good enough' or 'You don't deserve this'. This hidden belief can create behaviours that ruin your efforts. You might find yourself procrastinating on important projects, missing deadlines, or feeling like you're not putting in the necessary effort. It's like driving with one foot on the accelerator and the other on the brake.

Put Your Inner Critic on Trial

Another way to soften the voice of your Inner Critic and end the self-sabotage game is to decide whether it's fact or fiction by putting it on trial. To be convicted of a crime, there has to be sufficient evidence to prove your guilt. This is the exact process you should apply when you start telling yourself these self-defeating stories. Every time your Inner Critic feeds you that negative nonsense, put it on trial. Ask yourself: *Is there any hard evidence to support this story?* If there isn't, it's time to ditch it. And even if there is some evidence, who says the outcome will be the same next time? You'll be amazed at how many stories you've been carrying around with no real facts backing them up.

Let me give you an example. Have you ever had someone ask you to do something and your immediate reaction was 'Oh no, I could never do that', and when they ask why, you just say, 'I don't know, I just can't'? That right there is a classic case of a story with no evidence. If there's nothing solid to back it up, it's time to tell that story to jog on because the only person causing that limitation is you – and now you're aware of it, there is no excuse to let it keep playing out.

Here's another powerful way to empower your Inner Coach – investigate it. Let's say you spot someone you'd love to start a conversation with, but your Inner Critic kicks in, telling you that you'll mess it up, stumble over your words and make a fool of yourself. What do you think would happen if you ignored that voice, walked up to them, introduced yourself confidently, and walked away with the result you wanted? Your Inner Critic would take a serious hit, and your Inner Coach would feel pumped. You'd realize you don't have to believe every story your head tells you, and by proving it wrong, you can start eliminating more of the stories that have been holding you back.

Every time you prove your Inner Critic wrong, remind yourself of that victory and really rub it in its metaphorical face. Think about how wrong it was and all the benefits you got from ignoring its lies. Eventually, you'll start to recognize the same old stories popping up and be ready for them. You'll be able to anticipate their arrival and laugh them off. Like, 'Oh great, here comes the usual rubbish about why I should give up because I don't have what it takes.' But now, instead of holding you back, those thoughts will start to fade as your Inner Critic realizes it doesn't have the power to influence your actions any more.

It took three people telling me to write a book before I started writing this one. The first person was a friend about ten years ago. He told me I had so many stories that I could write an epic book. I laughed this off and dismissed it immediately, not even giving it a second thought. The second person was a coach who said, 'Lewis, you've got a book in you.' I gave it some thought but quickly dismissed it, making the usual excuses: 'I could never write a book', or 'Who would want to read my stuff?' I let the idea die again.

For the final time, I was approached for a book deal. That's when I knew I needed to examine what was holding me back. So I started asking myself questions. Have I ever tried to write a book before? *No.* So how do I know I can't? *I guess I don't.* Do I have stuff to write? *Yeah, I probably do.* Will anyone read it? *I won't know until I try.* That's when I decided to do an investigation, prove those stories wrong and start writing. Guess what? It turns out I can write a book. I've got a library of information stored in my head, and if you're reading this right now, then that means people did want to read it, so that's a win for my Inner Coach. My Inner Critic is left deflated, and my Inner Coach is yet again stronger than ever thinking about its next win!

Now, I wish I'd acted when my friend first suggested it ten years ago. But that's okay, it's not nearly as bad as someone who never realizes they're being held back by nobody but themselves. Don't let that person be you.

Topple Your Belief Bricks

But what do you do if you don't even know what's holding you back? Begin with a simple yet powerful question: *What are my recurring negative thoughts or beliefs about myself?* Write them down with raw honesty and without judgement. Next, ask yourself how these beliefs are showing up in your life. Are they influencing your actions, decisions or opportunities? Now, dig deeper. Where do these beliefs come from? Can you trace them back to specific events, people or moments? Was it a comment from a teacher or parent? The goal isn't to dwell on it; it's to pinpoint it.

Picture your limiting beliefs as a wall built from weak, crumbling bricks. Each brick represents a belief, assumption or experience you've stacked up over the years. Examining each brick, ask, 'Is this solid, or has it just been sitting here unchecked?' For every limiting belief you hold, there's usually an opposing truth waiting to tear it down. Let's say your belief is 'I'll never succeed because I've failed before'. The opposite truth is 'Every successful person has failed and it's just a step towards success'. Imagine placing this truth next to your limiting belief and watching it chip away at the wall. The more you reinforce the opposite truths, the weaker the wall becomes until it crumbles.

Try this: write down a limiting belief, then write the direct opposite next to it. For example, 'I'm not good enough' becomes 'I am enough, just as I am'. When you catch the limiting belief creeping in, immediately counter it with its opposite. This simple mental habit trains your brain to reject the negative and embrace a more empowering narrative, breaking the old one.

Joining the Stress Gym

Stress is another common trap that can be paralysing for many. Here's something to deal with stress that I like to call Stress Microdosing.

Imagine stress as your personal gym, but the weights are your challenges and each rep makes you stronger. We're not talking about bench-pressing your trauma just yet; we're starting small. Think of it like tiny hits of stress that build up your tolerance for the big stuff. Pick out situations that make you squirm a bit and start stressing out, like speaking up in a meeting or diving into that project you've been avoiding. Now, deliberately put yourself in those situations more often, and push yourself a bit further each time. Gradually, you'll start to notice that those nerve-racking situations don't have the same grip on you any more. You're not just putting up with stress, you're rewiring your brain to handle it – and every time you engage with it, you're sharpening your mental edges.

The Mental Flexibility Drill

Here's another way to alter your perspective of uncomfortable situations, using the Mental Flexibility Drill. Think of it as yoga for your brain and stretching those mental muscles that have been locked in the same patterns for too long. It's about getting your mind to bend, twist and move in ways it's not used to.

Think of a situation worrying you, or maybe you're procrastinating for fear of the outcome. Now, instead of letting the worry own you, take control by writing down three alternative ways to look at it. And listen, these don't all have to be sugar-coated, positivity-laced versions of reality – just different angles. The point is to train your brain to break out of its usual loop, and see things from perspectives that aren't trapped in the same tired narrative of the worst-case scenario – which, unfortunately, is how many people think by default. For instance, if you're up against a brutal deadline, and your brain is screaming, 'There's no way I can pull this off,' pause for a sec and consider these instead: 'This is a shot to see just how efficient I can be', or 'Maybe it's time to get smart about delegating'.

You're not just talking yourself into a better mood; you're rewiring your thought patterns, so when your brain tries to go down that same negative road again, it finds new routes. Why does this matter? Because the more you practise seeing things from different angles, the more you build up that adaptability muscle. And when life throws something unexpected in your path, you won't be stuck in a one-way thinking trap. You'll have options, and with options comes power.

Reprogramme Your Brain

You've already begun the journey of identifying your limiting beliefs and reprogramming them. Notice that word, as that is what you've just done: you've reprogrammed your brain using a simplified version of something called NLP (neuro-linguistic programming). NLP comprises a whole load of various techniques, but at its core is the idea that our thoughts, our language and our behaviours are all connected to each other and we can change them. As I'm sure you've worked out by now, I very much believe this to be the case – and in fact The Coaching Masters trains individuals to become NLP practitioners and NLP master practitioners. I've seen first-hand the transformative impact that this can have in changing how you perceive the world, as well as improving communication skills and emotional states, and even breaking phobias. I have watched it transform people's relationships and their lives. We'll look now at some key ideas that you can explore in your own life.

Anchoring Your Emotional State

A key one would be anchors and anchoring. This is essentially pairing an emotional state with a certain kind of stimulus. This might be a word, or a kind of touch, or a gesture, but you should make sure it isn't something you're constantly doing, as you might trigger it accidentally. A common example for an anchor would be touching your thumb to one of your other fingers. Once you have identified the emotional state you want to access – say confidence, relaxation or feeling motivated – then you need to find a strong memory where you felt like this, using all your senses to recreate it. Once you are really feeling it, then pair it with your anchor. You have to do this regularly and be consistent, and remember to use your anchor whenever you feel this feeling. Gradually, your anchor won't just reflect your state of mind – it will activate this state of mind.

Other people find that using anchors to interrupt negative thought patterns can also be useful. You can wear an elastic band around your wrist, and whenever you experience intrusive or negative thoughts, you can gently ping it. Then replace the negative thought with a positive affirmation, or a quick breathing exercise. This won't be a magic bullet. You will still need to do the deep work addressing where these negative thoughts are coming from. But in the short term, as a quick reset, it can work very well.

Swipe Left

Here's a fun trick that sounds ridiculous at first – but trust me on this. Have you ever been on a dating app? You see someone that's clearly not for you – maybe they give you the ick, or maybe they just remind you of your ex. Either way, you don't overthink it. You just swipe left. *Gone. Next.* No emotional drama. No three-hour internal debate. Just: *Not for me.* Now apply that to your thoughts. That negative voice that tells you you're not good enough? That unhelpful urge to scroll mindlessly instead of building your dream life? That old story you keep replaying about how 'people like me never succeed'?

Swipe left.

Actually do it. Physically. Stick your hand in the air and make the gesture. Throw that shit away like a bad Tinder match. Tell your brain: *This thought doesn't get my time today.* This links a negative pattern to a physical motion, so your brain starts to build new wiring around it. Over time, it creates a mental muscle memory. The more you do it, the easier it becomes to recognize and reject thoughts that don't serve you. Even better, once you've swiped left on the negative, replace it with something better. Don't leave your mental real estate empty. Choose the thought you *do* want instead. Confidence. Focus. Grit. Hope. Even if it feels fake at first, plant the new seed anyway. Negative thoughts will always show up, but you don't have to take them on a date, pour them a drink and let them move in. Acknowledge them. Swipe left. Move on.

This technique is playful, but powerful. You're training your brain to choose better. One swipe at a time.

Memory Rescripting

I want to help you use NLP for something more serious. What if some of those voices in your head aren't just made up? What if it's not your Inner Critic with a made-up story; it's a real event that you know exists in your mental landscape? What if I told you that some of these events in your life that you cannot seem to shake off, that keep you up at night, that weigh on your mind, that you try to numb with scrolling on social media or picking up a drink or whatever it is you use to get that picture out of your head – what if we could get you to laugh at them?

You see, the memory and the imagination are very similar, and it's often hard to tell the difference. Ever told a white lie for so long you can't remember if it's true or not? Well, that's your brain mixing things up in there. But we can use this to our advantage.

Painful memories can trigger negative emotions, limiting beliefs and self-sabotaging behaviours. By altering how you perceive memories, you can reduce their emotional impact and consequently the actions it leads you to take. What if you could change how these memories affect you? Through NLP, you can.

One particularly powerful NLP technique involves distorting painful memories – changing the sensory details of a memory to reduce its emotional intensity and negative influence on your present and future. Those nightmares from your past? You don't have to let them control you any more. We can scramble things up so they become so weak they can't touch you. This allows you to move past the pain, take control of your emotional response and create a different perception of the memory.

Let's get into it. Find a quiet place and close your eyes. Recall a memory that causes discomfort. Bring it to mind, focusing on its colours, sounds and emotions. Start altering specific sensory details of the memory. Imagine it in black and white instead of colour. Shrink the image down to a tiny size or move it far away from you. Change the sounds, making them faint or distorted, or even turn them into a funny cartoon voice. The goal is to make the memory less vivid and less emotionally charged. It's important to really play with and mess these memories up, because they will never be the same after. As you change these details, notice how the emotional intensity of the memory decreases.

Repeat this process until the memory no longer holds the same power over you. You might need to do this several times, but the memory should become less painful with each attempt. After distorting the memory, reinforce the new, less painful perception. Remind yourself that this altered version is how you now choose to remember the event. This helps cement the changes and reduces the likelihood of the old, painful version coming back to life.

Visualize and Manifest

Just as we can distort old memories in our imagination, we can visualize and manifest new empowering ones that not only make us feel better, but sometimes materialize into reality.

Imagine you've got a big speech to give at work. Start to visualize what the perfect version of it would be. Imagine walking up onto the stage, the spotlight on you. The audience staring back at you as you absolutely nail it. You hit every line; they laugh. When you finish, the applause is deafening. As you come offstage your colleague, bright eyed, tells you it was amazing.

When we visualize an event like this, various bits of our brains are activated – involving muscle memory, decision-making, and our emotions and motivation. Even though we're just imagining the event, this still strengthens our neural connections because of something called mirror neurons. For it to work, we have to try to add as much sensory detail as possible and do it regularly. We also have to combine it with actually doing the thing. But when we do, the impact can be enormous. Studies have found that adding visualization alongside physical exercise can actually make you stronger!

Take a few minutes daily to close your eyes and see yourself achieving your goals. Feel the emotions, hear the sounds and immerse yourself in the moment – make your brain feel like it's really there. This practice doesn't just keep you motivated; it programmes your mind to achieve what it believes.

This idea is closely linked to something known as the Law of Attraction, which is at the heart of things like *The Secret* and the manifestation trend. It's a belief that we can influence our reality through channelled intention, belief and visualization exercises. To boil it down: people who put out positive energy into the universe attract positive outcomes. I've always been wary of this because it feels too simplistic. We all know plenty of bad people who good things have happened to, and plenty of saints who've had terrible times. However, you don't necessarily have to believe in the magical vibration of magic energies, you just have to believe in the human brain.

There's something called the reticular activating system (RAS), which acts like a filter for what you notice in your environment. For example, have you ever bought a new car or a new pair of trainers and suddenly you see them everywhere? That's your RAS kicking into action. When you focus clearly on a goal, especially by visualizing it and attaching strong emotions to it, you train your brain to prioritize information and opportunities related to that goal. This focus influences your decisions and actions, creating a feedback loop which moves you closer to actually manifesting what you've visualized.

Whether magical vibrations, the human brain, or some combination of the two, all I know is that since I started putting positive thoughts and actions into the universe, it has come back to me.

There was one time when it went from being just a mental exercise to something that shook me to my core. I actually manifested a vision into existence exactly as I'd pictured it – but in a way that I never could've imagined. The funny thing is, life's got a wicked sense of humour when it comes to delivering what you need. It doesn't always show up how you expect, and it sure as hell doesn't always make sense at the time.

Back in 2018, I was auditioning for *Big Brother*. Yeah, the reality show. I threw my hat in the ring with an online application, got through the group auditions, met the psychologist, and even had a home visit. It was an almost year-long process, and I was flying back and forth from Bali for it. Then, boom – I got the call. I was in, and the show kicked off in less than a week. I was buzzing, beyond excited; I couldn't believe it. One of only twelve people who'd be locked in a house for the nation to watch, day in and day out, for three months. This was a dream for me, especially for that little kid inside who just wanted to be seen. So, how did I make it to the final twelve out of over 20,000 applicants? Every day, I'd play crowd applause music from YouTube, close my eyes, and imagine those sliding doors opening as I walked through with everyone screaming at me. I'd vividly see myself soaking up the cheers, my arms slightly raised, basking in the moment that I had made it.

But the excitement was cut short. A few days later I got another call telling me that the channel had rejected me at the last minute because of my criminal record. The production company had been willing to take the risk, but when it was crunch time the actual broadcast channel pulled out. The reality was, I was only three years out of prison for violent crimes. I get it now, but back then, it stung. It felt like my childhood dream of fame had been snatched away again.

But here's where the story takes a turn. That rejection? It made me throw myself into my business like never before. And just a year later, I was standing on a stage at my own motivational seminar. Three hundred people from around the world had flown in; we walked on hot coals, partied, and shared our stories. It was the first time I'd really bared mine onstage. And at the end of my speech, something surreal happened.

The crowd erupted into a standing ovation: cheers, screams, whistles, the whole lot. And then the event host walked up behind me and, out of nowhere, lifted my arms up as if to say, 'Take it in.' That was the moment it hit me. It snapped right into that visualization I'd played in my head for months. The universe, or maybe just my own mind, had delivered, but in a way I never saw coming. It was like life was saying, 'Reality TV isn't your path, Lew. You're here to change the world. But hang tight; you'll get what you want in time.' I'll savour that moment for ever.

When you rewrite your reality, you refuse to let your brain remain fixed. You open yourself up to growth and change. You transform that adversity you have faced from a static weight dragging you down to an opportunity to form new connections in your brain, the greatest asset that humanity has.

Key Takeaways

- You can change your mind. Not just your opinions, but the structure of your brain, through neuroplasticity.
- Learning how to develop a growth mindset will

maximize your chances of developing your abilities and intelligence.

- Concentrate on your Inner Coach, not your Inner Critic, which will transform how you experience challenges.
- You can reprogramme your brain using techniques from neuro-linguistic programming. This applies even to memories and your emotional responses to them.
- Visualizing success activates your mind to spot opportunities, and creates a feedback loop where belief, focus and positive action lead to real-world results.

Now you have brought together the work in the first two chapters of this book, you have essentially taken an audit of who you are at this moment and learned how you can make changes. This work is never done. I apply exercises from these chapters every day in my life. At this stage, though, we need to zoom out and look at what is going to motivate you at the very largest level as you do this work. We need to look at finding your purpose.

CHAPTER 3

Living with Fierce Purpose

Buzzzzz! Buzzzzz! Buzzzzz!

I jerk awake to my phone alarm and get straight out of bed. Exercise. Shower. Breakfast. Then I set off on my morning 45-minute bike ride. After so many days waking up with a head thick from vodka, dreading what the morning will reveal, or to the sounds of prison life, this kind of morning still feels like a kind of endless miracle.

I am twenty-six years old and finishing my first year of college. I have not missed a single class. Whatever the weather, I have ridden to my classes. I have started volunteering with two local charities. I am clean. I am sober. I am the healthiest and happiest I have ever been. Reborn. Cheesy as it sounds, but I can't think of any other way of putting it. The person I used to be feels as distant to me as a stranger. Most importantly, for the first time I have realized something key. Happiness is a distraction. If that sounds strange, let me break it down for you.

I'd left rehab the year before, and it was as if I had walked back into another world. My mind, which had always felt like a busy market square, full of noise and movement, was suddenly quiet and still. As soon as I was out, I began attending AA and NA meetings. I was living on meagre £50-a-week benefits, but I didn't mind at all. Previously, I had always been focused on making money, but for the first time in my life I had the peace to think about what I really wanted. Then I thought of Suzie's voice: 'Of course you can.' And I realized that I wanted to go to university. So my first step was to enrol on an access course at college, which would earn me the qualifications I would need to be able to apply for university. I knew this would be tough. My reading and writing skills had been weak when I left school. I would be in classes with people ten years younger than me, who had just come straight out of school.

Those early weeks at college were a constant reminder of just how much catching up I had to do. Simple things like how to structure an essay, how to reference books, how to use a library – things the others just knew how to do, I had to learn from scratch. I had never even been in a library before. The only book I had ever read was *Charlie and the Chocolate Factory* when I was seven years old. The old me, the one still telling the old stories, with a fixed mindset, would have focused on how unfair it was that they'd had this advantage. I'd have got angry. I'd have obliterated myself with booze and drugs, so as not to hear my dad's voice spitting 'you're a buffoon' at me. But all the work I'd done, in prison and then in rehab, had given me the strength not to do that. It allowed me to see everything I was intimidated by as an opportunity. Like someone starting from right at the back of the race, I decided I just had to run faster and harder than everyone else. So, I did.

I didn't waste time focusing on what I couldn't do. I started from the bottom of the mountain and I set off, climbing it step by step. And it turned out that I might not have known as much as the other students, but I was absolutely willing to work flat out to catch up with them all. And as I did, I started to feel good about myself in a way I never had before. The comments on my essays got better and better. I got my first bit of proper coursework back and was given a distinction. It happened on the next one too. Then I scored the highest mark in the college and won an award. I had spent my entire life certain that I was stupid, and that schoolwork wasn't for people like me, but there I was, pouring every single part of myself into what I was doing – and each day I learned a little bit more.

I was absolutely loving the process. And that's when I realized. Happiness shouldn't be the goal – it's the by-product of progress. Happiness is what happens when you find a way to live with fierce purpose.

The Happiness Myth

Let's break down this obsession with happiness that's been sold to us like some Black Friday offer promising everlasting bliss. Chasing endless happiness is not possible, and it just leads to frustration. Happiness is a fleeting emotional state. Chasing it is like trying to catch smoke with your bare hands. You'll never hold on to it for long. Society loves to tell us that happiness is the ultimate goal, but this endless pursuit leaves us feeling empty and as though something is missing, or questioning why we are not as happy as others. How many people do you know who are always chasing the next thing? The next promotion, the bigger car, the more exotic holiday. But does it make them happy? Or, once they get there, is there immediately another thing just over the horizon? I remember a prison psychiatrist hitting me with the simple line: 'Enjoy the journey, not just the destination.'

This mindset has carried me through everything since: rehab, building my business, all of it. Waiting for happiness is a trap that blinds us from seeing everything that happens along the way. We need to stop focusing on the things that are just over the horizon and focus on right now.

It's even worse in our social-media-obsessed age, as we scroll through carefully selected photos of other people projecting their happiness. Studies have shown that we look at social media more when we're unhappy. On top of that, the pressure of positive thinking is everywhere. Everywhere you look there are self-help books and motivational speakers telling you to 'choose happiness', and this creates an environment where any negative emotion is seen as weak. This pressure not only makes genuine happiness harder to attain, it also makes us feel guilty for not pretending life is 100 per cent amazing all the time. It's a cycle that leaves us even more unhappy. But this is because we're focusing on the how and what of the things we think will make us happy – not *why*.

Realizing Your Why

In his book *Start with Why*, author and inspirational speaker Simon Sinek sets out how there are three aspects to a business: the Why, the How and the What. Most businesses start with How or What. The truly great ones start with Why. As an example, you can imagine a version of Apple Computers that starts with What and How: 'We want to sell lots of our really good computers. They're easy to use and produce great results.' However, that's not how Apple does it. Instead, they start with their mission – to do things differently and change the world for the better – and the computers come from that purpose. In his follow-up book *Find Your Why*, Sinek applies these concepts to individuals.

At The Coaching Masters we have adapted an exercise based on these ideas. A warning: if you're doing this properly, it shouldn't be a cosy fireside chat. It's an interrogation where you're both the detective and the suspect. You need to keep going with brutal honesty, until you've peeled back all the layers of bullshit and excuses and you're left with the bloody, beating heart of your real motivation.

Your *why* is the reason you get out of bed in the morning – the core belief that drives you onwards. It will come from the life experiences that have shaped who you are. And once you discover it, you must live your life according to it and be true to it when you are making every decision.

Interrogate Your Why

Start with something you think you want. Let's say it's a promotion at work. Then just ask yourself: *Why?* Your first answer will be surface level. 'I want to get a pay rise.' Fine, but that's just the bait. Ask again. Maybe this time you say, 'Because I want security.' Dig deeper. *Why?* 'Because I want to feel safe.' Good, now you're getting somewhere. Ask yourself why five more times. Don't stop until you're uncomfortable. The goal is to get to the root cause, the thing you're avoiding because it's ugly, messy or hard to admit. Maybe it turns out that the real reason you want more money isn't about the money at all, it's about proving something to yourself or others – or maybe it's because you've got a deep-rooted fear of failure, thanks to some childhood trauma you've buried under layers of bravado. Do you just want the recognition that you have done well or that you are working hard? What you will often find, if you ask yourself why enough, is that you will discover the voids that have created your values.

How Voids Create Values

A few years ago, one of my mentors, Dr John Demartini – a world-renowned human behaviour specialist, international speaker, and author – told me that 'our unfulfilled past often creates values in our present', and suddenly what had been happening in that first year at college made sense. I had spent my entire childhood feeling that whatever I did, my dad would think I was stupid. I had craved love, safety, recognition and freedom. But I had spent the first part of my life looking for them in entirely the wrong way. I had surrounded myself with anger, danger and indifference. Perhaps I was hoping that someone would magically appear and give me the things I most needed if I showed I needed them enough. When I tried hard at my essay and got back good comments, it wasn't some small, surface thing; it was rooted deeply in my values. Working hard, receiving recognition, working harder, receiving more recognition – it was filling something that had been missing right at the heart of me. Voids create values.

The things we feel we lacked in the past become the fuel for what we value and strive for in the present. Our values aren't a cheap concept or motivational buzzword; they're the invisible blueprint for everything we do. They shape our decisions, influence how we treat people, determine what we'll fight for, and are pretty much the defining factor behind everything we do, whether we're consciously aware of them or not.

They're built over time, often through experiences, both good and bad; and they can change, sometimes gradually or sometimes in a moment of epiphany. Maybe you value kindness because you know what feeling dismissed or overlooked is like. Maybe you value adventure just because of the movies you watched growing up. Perhaps you value success because a book inspired you. You don't need to focus on where your values come from, but it is essential to become conscious of them so you can tie them to your decisions and make an anchor for your goals – once you do this, you will fall into alignment with where you really want to be in life. You're no longer pushing against the tide; you're swimming with it. When you're living in line with your values, things feel right and like you're walking your own path.

But when your actions clash with your values, that's when the inner conflict starts. You feel stuck, or frustrated, or like something's missing. And the worst part? Most people don't even realize what's causing it. But that won't be you – because we can start to uncover your values now.

Start by looking at the standout moments in your life. What made you feel unstoppable – like you were where you were meant to be? And what about the times that felt like everything was off, heavy or just wrong? These moments hold clues about your values. Think about the times you stood up for something or felt a sense of pride. What were you honouring in those moments? For example, if you felt proud of speaking your mind during a tough conversation, maybe honesty or courage is one of your values.

Now, think about what gets you excited. What do you spend your time and energy on, even when no one's paying attention? For example, if you organize group holidays or always bring people together for dinners, connection or community might sit high on your list. Or if you're obsessed with designing the perfect Instagram-worthy space at home, creativity or beauty could be a key value for you.

It's just as important to notice what irritates or frustrates you. That's often a sign your values are being violated. Maybe you can't stand when your ideas are brushed aside in meetings – that might mean respect or recognition is a big deal for you.

Pinning down your values might feel tricky at first, especially if this kind of introspection is new to you. To help you figure it out, imagine you have to cross out half of the values listed below, until you are left with the twenty that mean the most to you. Then cross out half of those until you only have ten:

Authenticity, Loyalty, Community, Ambition, Courage, Gratitude, Health, Education, Contribution, Dependability, Integrity, Generosity, Creativity, Family, Self-respect, Adaptability, Self-improvement, Individuality, Assertiveness, Supportiveness, Open-mindedness, Growth, Flexibility, Playfulness, Independence, Kindness, Honesty, Accountability, Balance, Teamwork, Curiosity, Self-discipline, Equality, Humility, Innovation, Joy, Optimism, Patience, Reliability, Respect.

Then aim to go further. Which one of those ten means the most to you? Which ones mean least? What are the eight, the four, you would keep? It might feel strange to do this at first, as we're so used to not thinking about this stuff with our conscious brain. Often we only perceive our values when they evoke an emotional response.

If you find it too limiting to use a pre-existing list, then you can develop your own by asking yourself a series of questions and noticing the answers that come into your mind.

Ten Coaching Questions to Uncover Your Core Values

1. What do I always make time for, no matter how busy life gets?
2. What would I be doing if nothing held me back – and what would that honour?

3. What kind of life would feel truly right to me?
4. What experiences have I had that I'm genuinely proud of?
5. What's something I keep avoiding but know deep down is important?
6. If I could change one thing in the world, what would it be – and why?
7. When do I feel most energized, focused or in flow?
8. What qualities do I admire most in the people I respect or love?
9. What principles do I hope my children (or future generations) live by?
10. If I had five years left to live, what would I change to make my life feel complete?

Don't rush through them. If a memory pops up, follow it. If one of the questions stirs a strong feeling, pause and sit with it. Any time a thought or insight comes up, jot it down. Nothing is too small or too random; it all matters.

Then step away for a day. Let your subconscious keep working in the background. If anything else surfaces, add it to your notes. When you come back, read over what you've written. Sit with it. Reflect. Then go deeper. Layer by layer, try to drill down into the essential core of what your answers are really telling you. What do they reveal about what you stand for? What patterns keep showing up? The aim isn't to overthink, it's to uncover. This process isn't about getting it right, it's about getting to something real. You're building your own personal values list, one that's been lived and felt.

Once you've got that list, start filtering. Refine it. Peel away the ones that feel nice but aren't truly yours. Strip it down until what you're left with feels undeniably you.

If you can boil it all down to one core value, this is your north star. It's the reference point for your decisions, for knowing what to walk away from and what to move closer towards. It's how you'll know you're walking in alignment with your values. Then you can ensure your actions are based on intention, not guessing your way through life or moving in a direction that might look 'right' but is actually someone else's path.

The Hero's Apprentice

An interesting way to uncover your values is to find five people you admire, real or imagined, and pick two qualities you respect from each. They don't have to be perfect; they just need to represent something you value. Then bring all those traits together to create your own version of a hero. Give that hero a name, maybe even an origin story if it helps. What would their journey look like? What have they overcome? Who would they stand up against? What do they fight for, and what do they never compromise on?

Now imagine you're their apprentice. You're about to be trained by them to step into their world and continue their mission. What would they need to pass on to you to do that properly? What would be the first five things they'd teach you? Not just skills, but principles. Truths. Values. Those things they live by that make them who they are. Write them down. They're likely the things you deeply resonate with too.

For me, one of those people is Steve Jobs. Not just because I'm into tech, but because of how fiercely he protected his vision, how relentlessly he chased simplicity, and how he didn't bend to fit in. When I hit a crossroad, I ask myself what he would do. Would he compromise on something just to be liked? No.

Would he prioritize creativity over approval? Yes. And if it feels aligned with who I am, I integrate those qualities into my own approach, my goals and the way I lead.

Sometimes this level of distance actually makes it easier. When you look too closely at yourself, it's easy to get stuck in the stories you've been told or the mental barriers you've built up over time. But when you look through the lens of someone you admire, the fog clears. You start to see what you really care about. And in that reflection, you often find yourself.

The You Award

Here's another quirky way you can uncover more clarity, if you take it seriously. Imagine you're getting an award. Not for success, or making money, or some surface-level thing – but for being the most *you* you've ever been. Real. Honest. Aligned.

Now here's where it gets interesting. The person stepping onstage to hand you the award isn't a celebrity or a role model you've always looked up to. It's you. The future version of you. The version who stopped people-pleasing. The one who finally said no to the wrong shit and yes to what actually matters. The version who's clear, consistent, and doesn't waste energy on stuff that doesn't align with their values.

That's what I do. I picture that version of me – not some fantasy, just the truest version of me who's doing what I know I'm capable of. He's not trying to impress anyone. He's just living with purpose. When I'm not sure what to do next, or I catch myself falling into old habits, I ask myself what would he do? And if the answer feels right, I use that as my next move. It's like having a filter for all the noise. So, take a minute and let that scene play out. Imagine them stepping up, taking the mic and explaining why you deserve the award. What do they say you've done? What have you stood for? What decisions did you make that changed the game? How did you treat people? What impact have you had?

Then imagine them handing it over to you – as if they're saying, 'It's your turn now.' That future version of you isn't miles away. They're built through small choices, made again and again, based on what actually matters to you. That's how you move closer. Not by dreaming, but by aligning.

Ten New Things

Most people say they want change but don't actually change anything. They stay in the same routine with the same habits and the same excuses. And they wonder why they feel stuck or directionless. Nothing new is going to show up in your life if you keep living on autopilot. So, here's something simple – but not easy. Try ten new things. Do them fast. Back-to-back if you can. The idea is to break your usual patterns and get some fresh data on what makes you tick.

Don't just do the obvious stuff. Stretch yourself. Go to a type of gym class you'd usually laugh at. Have a conversation with someone you don't usually talk to. Go to a workshop that makes you feel awkward. Take a cold plunge. Go to a spiritual event even if you're not 'into that stuff'. Say yes to something spontaneous. Travel without planning everything. Buy some clothes you've never worn before, either from a charity shop or your first designer label. The point is, you'll learn what feels most comfortable, uncomfortable, refreshing or icky – all of this is data that you can use to help uncover your values.

You're not doing this to become some new person. You're

doing it to find out who you already are when your routine gets disrupted. Because it's in those moments of unfamiliarity that your values start showing up. You'll notice what you care about, what energizes you, what drains you, what excites you and what definitely isn't for you. Even the things you hate will show you something, because you'll have to ask yourself *why*.

Radical Feedback

If you really want to figure out what you value in life – not just the stuff you tell yourself you value, but the values you actually live by, ask someone who's seen you at your worst. Don't go to someone who'll tell you what you want to hear. Go to someone honest. Brutally honest. The kind of person who respects you enough *not* to bullshit you. Ask them: *When have you seen me truly fired up – in a good way and in a bad way? What do you think I care about more than I let on? What do I stand for, even when I pretend not to?* Then shut up and listen. Because values aren't always pretty. They don't live on vision boards or in your Instagram bio. They live in what you defend. What you fight about. What pisses you off. What lights you up without warning. Sometimes we say we value success, but what we *really* value is recognition. Or we think we value peace, but we're always chasing intensity. These questions cut through all that. They force you to confront what's real – not what's curated.

Back in the day, if I'd asked my mates to do this for me, they'd probably have told me I was fired up by confrontation. By breaking rules and transgressing boundaries. And back then, this energy was channelled in all the wrong places. I was looking for a fight with everyone around me. But at my core, the desire to break through the limits that are imposed on us all – that's still in me. That's still the fire in the furnace. It's just I've learned how to channel it constructively. Your values are your compass, for sure. But if your compass is cracked, you'll keep walking in circles. This is your chance to recalibrate.

Brutal honesty. Radical clarity. That's where the real shift begins.

Three Photos

If sitting down to list your values feels like trying to name all the stars in the sky – don't. Some of us aren't wired to express ourselves in words. So you don't need to start with words. Start with what hits you in the gut.

Here's a different approach: for the next seven to ten days, take three photos a day. No filters. No doing it for the 'gram. Just take photos of what actually matters to you in that moment. It could be your kid sleeping on the sofa. The view on your morning walk. The coffee mug you use every single day. The book you keep coming back to. Your worn-out gym shoes. Whatever pulls something real out of you. Not what you think *should* matter. But what *does*. At the end of the week, sit with those photos. Lay them out in front of you, physically or on your phone, and ask yourself: *What do these things have in common? Why do they matter to me? What do they represent about the way I want to live? If I had to give a name to the feeling they trigger – what would it be?*

You're not just collecting images. You're reverse-engineering your values. Most people spend their whole lives chasing what they think they should want. It's too easy to absorb the same generic values or interests you see on the internet. These photos will help you cut through that. They'll show you what's already there in the background of your everyday life. This exercise isn't about pretty pictures. It's about working out the things that really matter to you in your everyday.

A You Tattoo

Let's take this further than taking photos – tattoos are images that define us in a way that words can't. If you already have tattoos, take a moment to really think about them. What are they of? What do they mean to you? Why did you choose them at that point in your life? Sometimes we get inked for fun, sometimes for pain, sometimes to mark a moment. But under it all, there's usually something deeper – a feeling, a memory, a part of who we are.

For me, I wouldn't have thought my tattoos *meant* anything at the time. I just liked how they looked, or they gave me a feeling I couldn't quite explain. But now, when I look back at them, it's clear there was something subconscious driving the choices. I've got locks and keys, skulls and angels, Greek gods, animals, religious symbols, cards, clocks, and taglines like *carpe diem* – the whole thing literally paints a picture of who I am. Even if I couldn't explain what each one meant at the time, I can look at them now and see they tell a story. My story.

If you don't have any tattoos, imagine you're about to get one. Not just a random design but the ultimate tattoo that represents you. Something that says: *This is what matters to me.* What would it be? What symbol, word or image would you carry with you for life? Do some research. Look at other designs, sketch something out – even if you're rubbish at drawing. Then write a short explanation of why that tattoo is so meaningful to you. It doesn't need to be deep or poetic, it just needs to be real. This exercise isn't really about body art. It's about becoming clear on what defines you at your core.

Purpose Retreat

Once you feel that you're gaining a better understanding of your true values, take yourself somewhere without any distractions. I'm not talking about a weekend spa break or putting your phone on silent for an afternoon. I mean really disconnect. Strip it all back. No phone, no people, no noise. Just you and whatever's left.

You can do this in your own space if you truly commit, but I know people who've taken it much further. Friends of mine have flown to India for Vipassana retreats. No speaking, no phones, no books. Just you and your thoughts, for hours a day, sitting in stillness. It's intense. Some people break down. Some crack open. Others emerge with a clarity they didn't know was possible.

There are places in Bali, too, where people spend days in complete darkness. Literally. No light, no distractions. They slide food to you through a hole in the wall and you sit in the pitch-black for a whole week. Nothing to do but face whatever's inside you. That might sound extreme, but some people swear that things come bubbling to the surface that just don't in day-to-day life. When you strip away all the noise and light and movement and distraction and it's just you and your thoughts, that's when something else, something new, has to take its place. Of course, you don't have to fly to India or lock yourself in a dark cave. We can all find ways to take a break from the noise of our daily lives. From our job, our mates, our routines. Maybe you could go camp alone. Take a day. Take three. Strip it all back and ask yourself: *What actually matters to me? What do I keep coming back to when no one's watching? What would I fight for, even if I lost everything else?*

It's going to feel weird. Pointless. Maybe even terrifying. But that's the point. If we can learn to make space for silence, if we can learn to listen to that voice whispering inside us and note down what it's saying, then we can uncover what really matters to us. It doesn't need to sound clever, or meaningful. You don't need to tell anyone else if you don't want. This is just for you. And it's when the real work starts.

For me, I don't know whether it was being physically locked up in prison or the mental prison I put myself in, but I discovered my number-one value is freedom. Freedom is the ability to say, think or do anything without barriers. It's the ability to have the things you want, spend time with the people you want to be with, and even live wherever you want. This is why I designed my business entirely online and surrounded myself with personal development communities. I get to constantly grow and create more freedom for my inner self, but I also get to travel and move from one country to the next by – as an ultra-minimalist – packing up my two suitcases of belongings and moving to my next adventure. Most people have no idea what their values actually are. They're just winging it, stumbling through life, wondering why something feels off or why they can't seem to stick to their goals.

At the same time as you begin to think about the values that most matter, you can also think more about the voids that may have led to your values. Ask yourself: *What did I feel was missing in my life growing up?* Think about moments you felt overlooked, unsupported or misunderstood. How does that gap still show up in your life today? Are there areas where you feel extra driven – or even sensitive – because of it? Could this be guiding you towards what you value most now? Do you think about anyone specific in your life when you begin to think about certain values? Do some people provoke an emotional reaction in the way that others don't?

As you begin to get a clearer sense of your values and how they were formed, you can begin to think about how to join up the present with the future you want. And here let me address something to help you out – before you dismiss it due to believing or feeling as though it's not a 'good value' to have. It's the elephant in the room for a lot of people, but it's essential in order to become unlimited.

It's time to admit something that can sometimes feel like a guilty secret. Maybe you want to be rich?

Why Being Rich isn't Bad

Let's be real for a second, deep down. Every single one of us wants to be rich. Not because we're greedy, and not necessarily because we want to flex or show off, although that's okay if that's your thing – there is nothing wrong with being proud of the accomplishments you've been brave enough to obtain for yourself if you discover materialism is your thing – but because being rich means freedom. My business partner Liam once called money 'freedom tokens'. That stuck with me. Because that's exactly what it is: tokens you can spend to do less of what you hate and more of what lights you up. Whether that's quitting a job that drains you, spending more time with your kids, travelling the world, or just buying yourself some breathing room. Money gives you options.

The problem is, we've been fed this idea that wanting to be rich is somehow bad. That wealth equals greed. That rich people are selfish, flashy, disconnected from the 'real world'. Sure, you'll see the guy in the Lambo revving his engine outside a club. But for every one of him, there are a thousand quiet millionaires funding charities, building schools, helping communities, or just living a peaceful, spacious life on their own terms. Rich doesn't have to mean showy. It doesn't have to mean 'better than'. It can just mean choice.

Let's break this down. If a woman in Africa uses money to install a system for clean water for her village, is she greedy? If a guy earns a fortune and uses it to put his mum in a better home, is he evil? If a filmmaker makes millions and finally gets to produce the story he's dreamed of since he was eight years old, is he a sell-out? No. They're just people who used wealth to fulfil a meaningful goal. 'Rich' is subjective, and once you realize that, it changes everything. The truth is that most people who claim they 'don't care about money' are either lying to themselves or protecting themselves. Maybe they've tried and failed. Maybe they're scared of what having money might say about them. Maybe they've picked up beliefs like 'money is the root of all evil', 'money doesn't buy happiness', or 'I just don't want to be greedy', from their family, culture or religion. But those beliefs don't protect you, they limit you. They trap you in struggle, while quietly judging anyone who breaks free from it.

Now, I used the word 'rich' because it's powerful. But when you zoom out, being rich isn't just about having a fat bank account. It's about having freedom – of time, opportunity, health, love, clarity, peace of mind. Some people are rich in spirit but poor in options. Others have all the options in the world but no idea who they are. But the ones who do the most good? They usually have both. Because when you're not in survival mode, you can actually help others survive.

The Power of Wealth with Purpose

Liam once shared a piece of personal advice he received from Paul McKenna, the British hypnotist, behavioural scientist and bestselling author known for his work in personal transformation. It is simple, but powerful: 'The more people you help, the more money you earn.' That one sentence changed Liam's life – and the second he told me, the same lightbulb switched on in my head.

You see, business is about solving problems. And the bigger the problem you solve, the bigger the compensation that will follow. That's the game. And when you figure out how to solve a problem at scale – not only do you help people, but you become rich in the process. Now, I know that word might make some people twitch. 'Rich'. But it shouldn't. Because truthfully, money only has a bad rep from people who don't have any. It's just another mental smokescreen – an unconscious rationalization that comes from limiting beliefs.

Some people tell themselves they don't want to be rich, but only because deep down they believe they never will be. And, for many, the real fear is what comes with it – responsibility, change, pressure, visibility. And as we've talked about before, your brain isn't wired for change. Even positive change triggers uncertainty, and your mind will avoid uncertainty at all costs.

But here's a truth no one can deny: you'll never hear a rich person saying they wish they were poor. Sure, they may eventually re-evaluate what matters to them, they may redefine success beyond material wealth – but they won't wish their money away. What you'll find instead is that once someone has more money than they could ever spend, they start using it to do good. In fact, the only people who *give away* that kind of wealth, on a world-changing level, are philanthropists. And do you know what some of the biggest philanthropists in history did to get their money? They were successful entrepreneurs first.

When people hear the word 'rich', the image that often comes to mind is one of excess – fast cars, designer clothes, private jets, and champagne-fuelled parties on yachts. But this surface-level perception misses the true potential of wealth. Real wealth is the kind that shapes the future. It's about having the resources and ability to create profound and lasting change. It builds hospitals where there were none, funds education systems in places where children have never had a chance, fights disease on a global scale, and even pushes the boundaries of what humanity is capable of.

Take Bill Gates, for example. After co-founding Microsoft and becoming one of the wealthiest individuals in history, he didn't just sit back and admire his fortune – he redirected his energy towards solving some of the most complex and devastating problems in the world. Through the Gates Foundation, he has committed over $50 billion to global health, sanitation and development initiatives. Gates has played a major role in the fight to eradicate malaria, improve vaccine distribution, fund clean-water projects, and prepare the world for future pandemics. He's not just writing cheques – he's building entire infrastructures designed to uplift communities and save lives for generations to come.

The legendary investor Warren Buffett has taken a similar path. Despite amassing a fortune of over $100 billion through smart, long-term investing, he has pledged to give away 99 per cent of his wealth to charitable causes. Most of it has already been distributed or earmarked for initiatives that combat poverty, improve education, and fund medical research. His commitment stems not from guilt or obligation, but from a clear belief that if you've been fortunate enough to be in the top 1 per cent of earners, you have a responsibility to think about the other 99. His philanthropic ethos is grounded in logic and compassion – he knows that capital, when pointed in the right direction, can save more lives than any speech or slogan ever could.

The pattern is clear. These are not people who got rich and only then decided to do something meaningful. These are people who understood from the beginning that, in order to change the world, they would need influence, leverage, infrastructure – and, yes, wealth. Because whether we like it or not, impact at scale requires resources. The kind of resources that can't be scraped together with goodwill and optimism alone. And this is the part people often miss. The idealist will say, 'We don't need money to make a difference.' But reality tells a different story. Try funding a clean-water initiative in Africa without money. Try building a school in a war zone. Try eradicating a disease without labs, scientists, supply chains and years of coordinated work. Try launching a rocket to Mars or creating a prosthetic that allows a paralysed person to walk again – without millions in R&D.

The reality is these things cost. Not just in terms of effort, but in hard, tangible capital. And the people who have access to that capital are the ones who are best positioned to lead change. That's why being rich matters. Not for the status or the superficial luxuries, but for what it allows you to *do*. Money gives you choices. It gives you freedom. But most importantly, it gives you the power to serve, to innovate, to build, and to lift others on a world-changing scale.

Can you name a single person who has truly changed the world on a massive scale without money? Because whether it's through the mind of a genius or the hands of a builder, the engine behind every world-changing movement has always been fuelled by resources. And those who dare to dream big, solve global problems and shape the future don't just need vision – they need capital to make that vision real.

That's why building wealth isn't selfish. It's essential. The more we earn, the more we can give. The more power we hold, the more lives we can touch. In the right hands, being rich isn't the end goal – it's the beginning of real impact. And if you want to help more people than you could ever meet in a lifetime, the first step is to create the means to do it.

Now we've started to explore your values, and maybe even planted the seed that wealth is important to provide the world with what it needs, imagine being able to put yourself and your purpose at the centre of it all? With *ikigai* you can.

The Four Pillars of *Ikigai*

In Japan there is a concept known as *ikigai*, which roughly translates as 'a reason for being'. It is often represented as the centre of four interlocking circles, representing what you love, what you're good at, what the world needs and what you can be paid for. In the coaching world, this is how we help people find their niche – a specific area of their skills to focus on that will help people and be in demand.

Take a moment to really absorb the power of what we are talking about here, whether it's coaching or some other occupation or business. Imagine doing something you love, that can be shared with the world, solves real problems and helps people on a profound level – and it has a value significant enough that people want to pay for it. Sounds like a dream, right? It's not. The lie that's been sold is to find a trade, get a job and stay safe – but millions of people have pushed past that and gone after what they *really* want. This isn't a dream, it's a reality; you just need to pay close attention to finding your sweet spot in the middle of your four circles – in other words, your *ikigai*.

Most of us spend our time on things that tick at least one of the boxes, but the compounding power for you, your income and the rest of the world comes from finding something that sits inside all four circles. It's such a powerful concept that, in some form, it's present all around the world, in all sorts of different cultures. In Ancient Greece it was known as *arete*, in India it is *dharma*, in South Africa it is *ubuntu* and in Finland it is *sisu*. Each of them has a slightly different emphasis but they all bring together the same idea. You've probably heard the phrase 'find something you love doing and you'll never work a day in your life'. But I have one that I believe fits better with my values, and probably yours too: 'get paid to be who you are, and work becomes freedom'.

This isn't some big abstract strategy. It is a way of finding purpose and joy in how we live a meaningful life in a practical, financially sustainable way. You may have heard the phrase, popular with the military, that 'how you do anything is how you do everything'. We need to find ways of expressing some aspect of our purpose in everything we do.

I was coaching a client once, someone who worked in a profession where attention to detail was key, who a couple of nights a month had to stay overnight away from his wife in the city. He told me that, to begin with, he'd buy a six-pack of beers and a kebab on the way home and fall asleep in front of the television. But it was making him really unhappy. Then he had a moment of revelation. Why was he treating himself worse than he would someone else? If he had a guest, especially someone he wanted to impress, there was no way he'd shove a takeaway in front of them. Part of his values was doing things properly, so behaving like this really didn't make sense. So, from that day on, he started treating himself like someone he wanted to impress. He bought fresh ingredients, he cooked himself a meal, he even bought a bottle of fancy wine. He brought attention to detail, care and effort to this small aspect of his life, and it transformed how he felt about it.

It can be very easy, when our lives tire us out, to take shortcuts and think we deserve time off. But this is the opposite of finding our *ikigai*. In the same way that going to the gym actually makes us feel less tired, finding a sense of purpose in the small things we do will energize us. If we see even the smallest of tasks as a way of expressing our purpose, then suddenly these tasks aren't such a pain.

When we start to analyse what matters to us, we bring back control over our lives into our own hands. We take ownership and responsibility for every part of our life.

Some of you may already know roughly what your *ikigai* is, but you've maybe not strategically thought about it in the context of this framework. Let's simplify things with four simple questions to ask yourself: *What do I love doing? What am I good at? Does the world need it? Would people pay for it?*

Let's look at a simple example. You love cooking and you're good at it. We know as a matter of science and society that everyone needs food and pays for it, so there is your *ikigai*. It's simple when you don't overthink it, isn't it? Now think about how many people love to cook, but are not only not being paid for it, but are in jobs they absolutely hate and that are not in alignment with their purpose. Why? Because they're waiting for a miracle or a sign from God to start moving.

Toxic Hope

What is the difference between optimism and hope? A lot of people use them pretty much interchangeably but they mean very different things. Optimism is a general belief that things will work out for the best. Hope should be specific and tied to your goals and your ability to achieve them. However, a great many people live their lives according to a general sort of non-specific hope that their lives will magically get better.

Always seeing the glass as half-full can be dangerous. A default optimism without a realistic assessment of your goals and capabilities as they are now can be as paralysing as relentless negativity. You can't just go out in front of an audience, sit down at the piano and hope that you'll magically be able to play something if you've never had a single lesson. It would be ridiculous to think this would happen. And yet so many people do this when it comes to getting the life they want. They fixate on the end goal and ignore all of the small essential steps on the journey. They're stuck in the quicksand of hope, slowly sinking while waiting for a miracle that will never come.

Hope can give us a false sense of security, making us think that the universe will somehow conspire to give us what we want just by wishing for it. But here's a hit of reality: it won't. Being hopeful in this way removes the responsibility from you just as much as blaming others does.

Using our earlier example, hope will never – and I mean *never* – make cooking part of your *ikigai*. And let's be real here: it can feel overwhelming or unobtainable if you are only thinking in terms of making your own cooking channel, opening up your own restaurant, creating your own brand of cookies or working for Gordon Ramsay – but that's looking at something entirely different. What you're doing there is dreaming of ultimate success.

Now, don't get me wrong, that's brilliant if you're ready to take action. Because if you do, eventually you will still find success. Here is the cheesiest quote you'll ever read, but I'll let it go as it fits too perfectly not to use it. Here it is: 'Shoot for the stars, and if you miss, you'll fall gently on the clouds.' Even if you go for the big thing and you miss, *ikigai* doesn't have a fixed point of success. You're successful if you're living your purpose, even if you haven't achieved it yet. As long as you find yourself sitting at the meeting point of those four circles on the Venn diagram, you're hitting every part that matters. It could be as simple as getting a job as a chef. Are you doing what you love? *Check*. We've already established you're good at it. *Check*. Does the world need it? *Check*. Will people pay for it? *Check*.

So, throw out hope and start moving. Hope without action is just procrastination dressed up as positivity. You don't need to wait for your dream life; you need to create it. And the crazy part? It's way closer than you think. You could be four weeks away. That's it. Four weeks. One job offer, a resignation letter, a notice period. That could be the distance between you and a completely different life. The kind of life where you wake up and feel like you're actually doing something that matters – something that feels like *you*.

Start now. Because once you're in motion, things will happen. Opportunities show up. People notice. Your confidence grows. The idea for the cookie brand? The cooking show? The restaurant? That all becomes possible when you're no longer standing still. *Ikigai* doesn't live in a fantasy world. It lives in action. You don't arrive there after ten years of waiting – you feel it the moment you start doing what you love, what you're great at, what the world needs, and what people will pay you for, at *whatever* scale, So, stop hoping and start doing. Keep going – and I can promise you, if it's in alignment with your values, the rest will follow.

Progressive Realism

At this stage, you've started to look at yourself, at your deepest motivations and values, and you have a clearer sense of your ultimate why. Now you need to make sure you're being realistic. Realism doesn't mean being negative, but instead facing the hard truths and making plans based on them – not on wishful thinking. Think about it. If you're always optimistic, you will likely be blindsided by setbacks. You're unprepared for the curveballs life will throw at you. But if you adopt a more realistic approach, you're ready for anything.

Take the business world, for example. Companies that operate under the assumption that everything will always go smoothly are the ones that crumble at the first sign of trouble. But those which plan for failure, anticipate challenges and have contingencies in place are the ones which survive and thrive. It's not about expecting to fail but about being ready for it, and okay with it *if* it happens. It's about building resilience through realism, not through false security. The application of hope keeps us in denial and wastes time. Hope often blinds us to reality. It whispers sweet nothings in our ears, convincing us that things will improve just because we want them to. Delusional hope keeps us stuck.

So, the next time you find yourself clinging to hope or optimism, ask yourself: *Is this hope driving me forward, or is it holding me back? Is my hope allied to action, or is it stopping me doing things?*

This next exercise will help you reflect on where you might be clinging to hope or optimism in ways that are holding you back – and guide you towards reclaiming control over your life instead. The goal is to identify areas where action and realism are needed to shift your mindset and start making tangible progress.

Analyse Your Hope

Step 1 – Reflect on your hope. What areas of your life are you currently 'hoping' will improve? Be specific: is it a relationship, career, finances, health, or something else? Ask yourself honestly: *What actions am I taking to improve this situation, or am I relying on the belief that things will improve on their own?*

Step 2 – Question your optimism. Think about a time when you were overly optimistic about something, and it didn't go as planned. How did that experience affect you? Are there situations in your life where you might ignore warning signs or avoid preparing for setbacks?

Step 3 – Embrace realism. What hard truths about your current situation have you been avoiding? What's the worst-case scenario, and are you prepared for it? What's the best-case scenario, and what realistic steps can you take to make it happen?

Step 4 – Shift the power. Reflect on areas where you've been giving your power away, whether it's to a person, a circumstance or even your own excuses. What would it look like to take back control in these areas? What's one action you can take today to reclaim your power and become confident in knowing where to move next in life?

This exercise isn't about letting go of hope entirely, but pairing it with action. It's about recognizing where you've been stuck in cycles of wishful thinking – and taking steps to move forward. Remember, true control doesn't come from waiting but from doing.

Purpose over Happiness

To bring this all together, I will hit you with an exercise we run at The Coaching Masters. It's a mindbender, but it's very powerful. Before we dive in, let me warn you that it's not for the faint-hearted. Some people find it hard to think about. But we've seen time and time again that it can unlock a level of clarity most people spend their whole lives avoiding. This exercise is a scary but effective way to dial down the noise, figure out who you really want to be, and decide the legacy you want to leave behind. Ready?

Imagine you've died, but you get to sit in on your own funeral. You are eavesdropping on what people are saying about you. What's in your eulogy? What do they remember? And here's where it gets even heavier: a year later, you're back at your grave, staring at that cold slab of stone. What does it say? What words are etched there, summing up your entire existence? Grab a piece of paper, sketch out your own tombstone, and carve out a sentence or two of how you'd like to be remembered on leaving this world. That's your ultimate self. That's the version of you that made it. Now, the real challenge is to spend every day becoming that person. Simple? Maybe. But damn, it's powerful.

So, what's the takeaway? Dig deeper. Ask why until you get to the core of it all. Once you know your true why, you'll stop wasting time on the things that don't matter and focus on what does. Then, figure out who you really want to become and what you want to be remembered for. And that, my friend, is how you take control of your life and future – by knowing what you're fighting for each and every day.

You Deserve to Dream

Finally, because that might feel a little bit too morbid, I want to finish this chapter with something really important. It can sometimes feel like growing up is a process of learning to let go of your dreams. Remember how you felt when you were a kid? You almost certainly had enormous hopes and aspirations. You wanted to put a dent in the universe. As we grow up, most of us revise our dreams downwards in size. This is completely understandable. Life can throw so many challenges our way. The day-to-day grind of a job, a relationship, a house, a family, never mind those nagging negative voices we all have – it can all drown out our dreams. But those dreams haven't disappeared. They're still there. The tombstone exercise is just an exercise. You're not dead yet. You still have the opportunity to transform what you will be remembered for, starting right this moment.

It's easy to convince ourselves that our current situation is all we can achieve. That somehow dreams are childish and that we're being grown-up by not having them. But so often I have seen how it is the dormant embers of a dream from childhood that are brought back to flame. The first step towards your dreams is the hardest one of all. Because it takes a huge amount of bravery to admit that you still have them. The good news is that you can start right now.

What is important is to separate the element of external validation from our dreams. When we're kids, of course, we want the biggest, the best, the fastest, the strongest. And we often equate that with being so good at something we become famous. But we need to stop looking for that outside validation and find the element of our dreams that will fulfil us from within.

You might not ever play up front for England, like you

dreamed, but you definitely could start playing five-a-side once a week. You might not be as big as the Beatles, but you definitely could take up the guitar and write your own songs. Your dreams are still there – and they still have the capacity to make you feel fulfilled in ways you can't yet imagine. Your dreams, those things you've always wanted to do, are within reach. They're not gone. They're just waiting for you to find them again. Yes, it might take some effort, and there will be challenges along the way, but you owe it to yourself to go after what truly sets your soul on fire.

I have seen, time and time again, when I interview those on my podcast who have faced the greatest adversity, they are then forced to work out what really matters to them. So many of the old patterns of their life have been disrupted. Often they are coming to terms with an entirely new physical reality, through illness or injury. But it is in facing this fundamental reconfiguration of their reality that they come to an understanding of what truly matters to them. And once they have that, they can move forward with an unstoppable force. They start charities, foundations or businesses that allow them to connect their purpose with their career – and it becomes their vocation. I see those who have been through this process not as unlucky, or people who are to be pitied, but people to be admired and emulated.

127 into 700,000

On 26 April 2003, the mountaineer Aron Ralston was solo canyoneering in Bluejohn Canyon in Utah when a boulder he jumped onto was dislodged and trapped his right arm against the canyon wall. For five long days he survived on the food and water in his backpack, and even drank his own urine – it's all recreated in *127 Hours*, which is a cool movie, I'd recommend it. Anyway, thinking he was going to die, he took out his camcorder to record a goodbye message to his family. As he mused on what he wanted to say to them, how he could communicate his deep love for them, he realized this wasn't the end. He improvised a tourniquet and broke both of the bones in his arm, then cut his flesh using his multi-tool knife. Over the course of the next hour, almost blacking out from the pain, he amputated his own arm. Then, with one arm, he rappelled down the 65-foot drop and hiked seven miles until he was picked up by the emergency rescue services.

Over the course of those 127 hours, Ralston faced a situation that none of us can imagine. But in that time he found his why. His family were what allowed him to complete an almost superhuman series of actions and return to tell them in person how much he loved them. The average lifespan of a person in the UK is 700,000 hours. If we can all find a way to apply some of the radical honesty Ralston applied in those 127 hours in our 700,000, then there is no limit to what we are capable of. And the best news is, you don't need to cut your arm off and drink your own urine to do it; you just need to give yourself a wake-up call now rather than ending up in a desperate situation where you're forced to take drastic action – or worse yet, never doing it at all.

Living with fierce purpose is about finding the balance between hope and realism, the pain of your past and the possibility of your future. The exact balance will be different for everyone. But the result will be that you wake up each day with a clear sense of direction and know what you need to do to get there. When we live with fierce purpose, any adversity that we face can't help but be an asset – because it is creating the environment where growth happens. And growth is the ultimate asset.

Key Takeaways

- Don't get hung up on happiness; make purpose your goal. Find your why. If you don't know it yet, you can ask yourself the right questions to discover it.
- Our values are very often formed by our past. Paying attention to this will help you find your true values so you can live your life in alignment with them.
- Being rich is not greedy – it's about freedom. Money gives you choices: to say no to what drains you and yes to what lights you up.
- Most people don't fear money – they fear what it might mean. Limiting beliefs like 'money is bad' or 'I'm not meant for that' hold people back more than poverty itself. True abundance starts by dismantling those inherited stories.
- Wealth fuels world-changing impacts. From hospitals to climate solutions, big change needs big resources. It's needed if you truly want to serve on a massive scale.
- Beware of toxic hope. A reliance on things magically getting better in the abstract can be as bad for you as relentless negativity.
- Your dreams aren't gone. They're buried under the noise of life. Responsibilities, doubts, and that voice saying you've lost them.

We've seen that life starts to shift when we stop blindly chasing happiness and start asking better questions – the ones that actually mean something. Figuring out what drives you, what lights you up and what your life could look like when you're in alignment with your values isn't just about finding purpose, it's about taking back control. That's a big part of what it means to be unlimited – breaking away from the scripted path and creating one that fits *you*.

But even when you know what you want, something still holds most people back: fear. Fear of failing, of being judged, of getting it wrong, or even of getting it right. So next, we're diving headfirst into fear. Not how to avoid it or pretend it's not there, but how to face it fully – because freedom doesn't come from feeling fearless, it comes from learning to move into fear and making it and discomfort your friend.

CHAPTER 4

Making Fear Your Friend

'Hi, my name's Lewis. And this is my story . . .'

A sea of faces stares expectantly back at me. I swallow, my throat suddenly dry. 'No one wants to listen to your shit,' a little voice in my head says. 'You're a *buffoon.*' I have absolutely no idea what is going to happen next. All I know is that suddenly this feels like the last place in the world I want to be.

Over the last year or so, I had begun to make some big changes in my life. I had kept attending AA and NA meetings where I'd seen people just like me turn their lives around. I'd seen how transformational the twelve-step programme could be. The twelfth step always felt so important to me – 'Having had a spiritual awakening as the result of these steps, we tried to carry this message to alcoholics or addicts and to practice these principles in all our affairs.' It wasn't just about focusing on myself. It was about helping others and creating a cycle of support and growth.

One day, I thought, *Why don't we have something like this for people who aren't addicts?* It felt like so many of the tools I had been developing in prison, in rehab and now at these meetings could be so useful to people who weren't addicts. I had tried before to launch a project called Hunger Start, to help people start their hunger for life, set and achieve goals, and feel supported. Unfortunately, it got a very lukewarm response. So I decided to be more proactive. I reached out to people in my local area on social media, offering to help them one-to-one with whatever they needed – setting goals, boosting self-esteem, anything – for six weeks. If they found it worthwhile, they could join the community. Six weeks of coaching for a potential £30, and I would buy the coffee. But that time and coffee expense turned out to be one of the best investments I could have made. In those six weeks, I made a real impact on quite a few lives, and that's where it all started.

It hit me like a ton of bricks. I'd been handed this incredible gift: the ability to help others break through the mental roadblocks I'd battled my whole life. During rehab in prison, six months of full-time rehab outside the gates, and months of daily AA and NA meetings, I'd heard hundreds of people's stories. Emotional confessions, real breakthroughs, deep blocks, painful relapses. And it gave me a level of insight that very few people ever get the chance to experience. Their journeys, along with everything I'd learned in rehab, counselling, treatment and from others, plus my own path – psychotherapy, psychiatry, even my time in prison doing my own inner work and creating my own transformational exercises just to survive – it all came together as one superpower.

I'd developed this deep, grounded understanding of how the mind works. I knew exactly what it was like to be stuck in that dark hole, but more importantly I knew how to get out. And I was already using that to help people. This wasn't the kind of learning you get from a textbook. It was real. Lived. I realized I'd had the world's best life coaching training without even knowing it. Every time I spoke to someone, I didn't need to refer to a manual or try to remember a class I once took. I just knew. I could feel where they were and talk them through it, step by step, because I'd been there. I could see it clearly, and they could feel that. That's when I knew I'd been given something powerful – something that wasn't just for me. And as clichéd as it sounds, I remember thinking: *If I can do it, anyone can.* And once you've felt that kind of transformation, and the belief that comes with it, you can't keep it to yourself. I couldn't shut my mouth. I wanted to help everyone with everything, and like magic, nine times out of ten, I could.

The next thing I knew, I earned an online coaching certificate. I'll never forget my first client – £600 for a twelve-week programme. I was so hyped that I literally jumped on my bed. Every penny I made, I reinvested in better tools and training. I was changing lives, and word was spreading. But I knew I needed to do more and get my message out in front of more people. So I put on my own event called Fire Up. Three hundred people from across the globe flew in from the community I was creating, and it was my time to fit the little parts of my story into one message that would lay my soul bare. Even if that meant facing my fear.

Fear Itself

Fear is one of the most powerful feelings there is. It's your brain's way of trying to keep you safe. And for good reason. Being afraid of the right things has been incredibly important at an evolutionary level. It's a very good way of surviving and passing on your genes. And the simplest way of being afraid of the right things is to have a very sensitive set of equipment for feeling fear. The problem is, that system is then very easy to set off.

Imagine you're walking down a dark street alone late at night, when suddenly out of the corner of your eye, right next to you, something moves. Immediately, before you've even realized what's happened, the part of your brain called the amygdala – part of your body's stress response system – activates. Hormones, including adrenaline, are released – making your heart beat faster and your senses sharpen. The blood starts flowing to your muscles, which tense in anticipation, and your breathing quickens. You turn to the side, your fists raised. The fox trots off, oblivious, to explore another bin. You laugh, hold your hand to your heart, shaking, amped and ready for action you don't need to take.

We all recognize what is known as the fight-or-flight response, our body's raw, chemical response to potential danger. What we perceive as the emotion 'fear' is closely bound to this. The problem is that this system, designed for a quick response to a simple threat, is still all we have to deal with the infinitely less dangerous situations that modern life produces. Instead of being chased by the tiger that once upon a time we may have had to deal with, what triggers this same fear response is often something that's been blown completely out of proportion – like sending a message to a stranger, or posting something on social media and worrying about what people will think of us. Fear shapes our entire lives. Studies have shown that we remember negative experiences more accurately and vividly than positive ones. More than that, those negative memories can cause us to feel afraid of situations that are only vaguely similar. Our fear essentially infects the surrounding memories.

There is a theory that so much of the global anxiety epidemic can be traced to our bodies triggering the flight-or-fight response in situations that response wasn't ever meant to deal with. Like an overly sensitive smoke alarm that gets set off by the steam coming off your cup of tea, we're in constant low-level fight-or-flight mode.

At a fundamental level, most people organize their lives to avoid doing things that make them feel scared. And often that's perfectly sensible. We all want to live lives with all of the needless stress removed. We don't want to worry about paying bills, or where our next meal is coming from. So arranging our lives to make that lack of stress happen is almost always a really good idea.

The problem is that, very often, a small amount of short-term discomfort is necessary for long-term gain. Like pulling out a splinter, or ripping off a plaster, you need to take that small hit for the long-term benefit. The motivational speaker Les Brown puts it clearly when he says, 'If you do what's easy, your life will be hard, and if you do what's hard, your life will be easy.' So often it is fear of the unknown, allied with wanting to avoid discomfort, that shapes our decisions.

Fake Fear vs Real Fear

Let's get one thing straight. Not all fear is fake. If you're walking down a street in Mexico City and a pack of wild dogs comes around the corner, I don't want you to ignore them. But so much of the fear that we feel day to day isn't real. It's fake fear. Fear of failure, fear of making the wrong decision, fear of being right, fear of being wrong, fear of judgement, humiliation, embarrassment, change or even success. What your brain is actually scared of in all these scenarios is the same thing – uncertainty and change. Your brain likes it when things stay the same, because it can then apply the same things to the same situations and get the same predictable results – safety.

Again, this makes total sense in an evolutionary context. If you stay in the same place, with the same people, you minimize danger. You know which plants and berries to eat, which animals to hunt. You know who you can trust. You know which watering holes to avoid and when. Change threatens all of that, as you have to learn a whole new set of rules, which leaves you vulnerable.

But again, the problem is that we're using a response designed for one thing to try to deal with another. There is very little danger that you are going to be eaten by wolves if you take that new job. Of course, in most situations there is a worst-case scenario that could result in a kind of harm. That piece of negative feedback on your work could technically lead to you losing your job, not being able to pay your mortgage, and having to live under the bridge and talk to a pigeon called Gerald. But, it's really, really unlikely. There are a huge number of steps you can take to avoid it. And it certainly isn't happening now. What you're doing is called catastrophizing.

What this means is that you are essentially borrowing worry from a fictional future. And the problem is, that source of fear is almost infinite. By the time you've reached the future and the worst possible thing hasn't happened, it's not like you just breathe out and feel fine. It's on to the next set of unlikely things to worry about. Especially today, in our always-on, constantly plugged-in world, we are overloaded with things to worry about. And not just in our own lives. We are constantly aware of huge, terrible global news stories. When we are feeling overwhelmed, we may try to avoid looking at the news.

But what your brain hates most is uncertainty. When we bury our head in the sand about something we fear, it actually makes it worse, because the version our brain comes up with is inevitably so much worse than the reality. The good news is that fear can be incredibly useful, if you learn how to channel it. Remember when we were talking about fight-or-flight earlier? Well, fear can equip you to do things, if you choose to. Up there on that stage, as I swallowed with a dry mouth, I realized something. Those butterflies in my stomach that I was interpreting as dread were exactly the same as the butterflies of excitement and anticipation. Think about it – why do people love horror movies and roller-coasters? Because fear in a safe environment, where you know it's not real, can be great fun. So all you have to do is help your brain recognize that your fear isn't real – and that fear will become something that fuels and energizes you, not drags you down.

False Evidence

Here's a useful acronym you may have seen flying about the internet – F E A R is False Evidence Appearing Real. This is a key point in helping to convince your brain that it's feeling fake fear. Remember that it only *appears* real. So far, we've looked at ways you can start to dig deeper into what you're actually scared of.

Let's take a really small example. Do you ever have that feeling when you're about to post something on social media – a silly photo, or even a joke or comment – and you pause for a moment with a flash of panic? You suddenly play out a scenario where people you care about hate the post. Maybe you imagine the mean things a hater would say. Suddenly this post provokes a feeling of dread. Something so small on its own starts to stand in for every time you've been rejected, or laughed at, or made to feel small. Every time you've ever felt like you aren't smart or interesting or lovable. Every time you've ever felt you're not enough. And your brain is trying to protect you from that bad feeling, so it tries to avoid posting the picture or comment. Again, in an evolution-ary context this makes sense. The positive opinion of our tribe is incredibly important. It could be the difference between life and death. We have evolved to massively care what other people think of us, and to tell others what we think of them. Of course, we're not forming hunting parties and going after big beasts any more.

For almost all of us, the stakes have massively shifted. But the feelings haven't. Today, your 'tribe' might be your followers or your social circle, but the fear still feels real – although in today's world, it's simply an illusion. The world won't end if your post on social media gets ignored. Your worth isn't tied to how many likes or comments you get. Fear only holds power if you let it, and the truth is, *you're* the one in control.

So, what do you do about it? Start by getting specific. Don't let fear stay vague and shadowy – pin it down. Ask yourself: *What exactly am I afraid of?* Is it a specific person seeing your post? Is it the fear of stumbling over your words or coming across as less polished? When you name your fear, you take away some of its power. Then, you can flip the narrative. Instead of asking yourself *What if this goes wrong?* try asking: *What if this can help someone?* What if your post inspires, connects, or opens up a conversation?

Finally, remind yourself of this truth. You are safe. You are enough. You are loved. Your value isn't determined by how others react to you. It's intrinsic, unshakable and, most importantly, yours. The more you internalize that, the less power the fear has over you. It's not about eliminating fear itself. It's about feeling it, understanding it and choosing to act anyway. So the next time you feel that familiar wave of doubt, take a deep breath, hit the post button, and know that by doing so you're reclaiming your power, one small act of courage at a time.

The FEAR Exercise

Here is an exercise using FEAR as an acronym, but this one is a model to diminish fear's effect on you and leave you in a cycle of actively embracing it.

Find: This is where you get specific. What exactly are you afraid of? Don't just leave it as a vague feeling of dread – dig in. What is it about this situation that's triggering you? Is it the fear of looking stupid, failing, or something else? Write it down, talk it out, and even draw it if that works for you. The clearer you are, the less room fear has to play tricks on you.

Embrace: Instead of pushing the fear away, lean into it. Imagine the absolute worst-case scenario in vivid detail. What if it actually happened? Would it destroy you, or could you deal with it? By the way, the answer is always going to be that you'd deal with it. By accepting the fear instead of resisting it, you'll start to see it for what it is – just another hurdle you can overcome.

Act: This is where things get real. Fear hates action, so taking even the smallest step forward dismantles its grip. Decide what that step is, when you'll do it and how you'll celebrate when it's done. Don't overthink it – just do something.

Review: Look back and ask yourself if the fear was as bad as you'd imagined? What did you learn? How did it change you? Reflecting on the experience helps you see how far you've come and prepares you for the next time fear tries to creep in. This process isn't about magically eliminating fear – it's about showing you that fear doesn't get the final say. You do.

What's the Worst Thing That Could Happen?

Here's another little exercise you can do the next time you're feeling anxious about a situation in your life. You can do this on your own, or it can be fun to do with someone you trust.

Start with the thing that's causing you to feel fear and ask yourself: *What's the worst thing that could happen?* So, if you have a presentation to do tomorrow that you're dreading, what's the worst version of it? And if it happens, what then? Maybe your boss is disappointed and gives you some feedback that you need to prepare better for presentations. So what's the worst thing that can happen after that? You ignore the feedback and the next one goes even worse. So, what then? Keep going, again and again, following down the worst-possible path each time. At every stage, as you plot out this series of terrible events, something magical will happen. It will start to feel funny. The sheer number of unlikely things that will need to happen, the number of times you and everyone you know would have to act in a way that is nothing like the way you would actually act, will start to seem absurd. And as soon as you laugh at fear, it's not fear any more.

Some biologists believe that laughter originally evolved as a response to signal that danger had passed. We all know this from our own lives. If someone scares you by creeping up on you, after the initial fight-or-flight response it's so often laughter that comes next. The good news is that you can reverse-engineer this. Finding a way of laughing at fear will make you feel less afraid. Because if you don't learn to laugh at fear, it will be laughing at you, and I know that you don't want your life to seem like a joke.

Your Fear isn't Always Yours

It's also important to remember that other people are driven by fake fear too. It might be your mum, dad, partner, childhood pal, or even your dear old nan. And this fear might drive them to do things that harm us. They try to put us in a cocoon to protect us, which sometimes means they crush our aspirations without meaning to. They plant seeds of doubt that can steer us away from what we really want. Sometimes they may even be projecting their own insecurities onto us. It might feel better for them if you avoid change like they have, because in a way it reinforces that they were right to.

One constant example I'm always hearing about is with changing jobs or leaving to set up your own thing. The world of work has changed massively in the last thirty years. The old model of joining a company and working your way up just doesn't apply for most people. They jump between companies, roles and industries, and from being employed to self-employed, owning their own business or some mixture of main and side hustles. But most people from the previous generation have that old model still in their heads. Their instinct will always be to stay where they are, to try to get ahead on the same path, to fear the unknown. Your side hustle may not even sound like a job at all to them, so of course they advise you to stay in a workplace you're not happy in. The problem is that it's like they're trying to navigate an ocean with an out-of-date map. They mean well, but they're not working with the best information.

If we're feeling scared of change, we're often looking for an excuse to stay where we are, so all it takes is one person to express hesitation and we leap on it.

Fear of Failure

What is failure? We all think we know. One of the things that often holds us back is the thought that we won't be able to do something. That we'll get it wrong. That we'll fail. I want to begin explaining the reality of failure with two stories.

The first is about a guy in 1985 who got fired after a massive disagreement with the board of the computer company he co-founded. He was accused of pushing his colleagues and employees too hard, and after two new products he'd championed had underperformed he was unceremoniously fired.

The second is about a guy who wanted to draw cartoons. He had arrived in Hollywood in 1923 with $40 in his pocket, having been sacked from his local newspaper for a 'lack of imagination'. He thought he had found success when he came up with a breakthrough character, Oswald the Lucky Rabbit. Only for his distributor to steal the rights to it, leaving him with nothing.

You may recognize both of these stories, but if you don't: the first is Steve Jobs. He went on to found NeXT, and when that company was acquired by Apple he ended up eventually becoming CEO and led Apple to becoming one of the most valuable companies in the world, creating the iPod, iPad and iPhone along the way. The second is Walt Disney who, without Oswald the Lucky Rabbit, had to settle for a character called Mickey Mouse. And we all know what happened there. If you had stopped their stories at the points mentioned above, both would be considered failures. But you only have to let their stories run and they become two of the biggest successes in history.

It's not a new point that many who are successful have faced adversity. I've read a *lot* of autobiographies and biographies about the highly successful, and it is incredibly common. The people who do great things don't do them straight away, and the path that led them to greatness is almost never a straight one. You could almost say you wouldn't have had the success without the failure. Walt Disney once said, 'A kick in the teeth may be the best thing in the world for you.' Steve Jobs described being fired as 'the best thing that ever happened' to him. Let's look now at some more famous 'winners'.

Now, I'm no sports fan. My heroes are pretty much totally from other walks of life. But sport is one area where winning and losing is pretty exhaustively recorded, and this allows for some interesting analysis of the statistics.

Sir Alex Ferguson, considered to be one of the greatest football managers of all time, had a win percentage across his career of just under 60 per cent. Michael Jordan's was 66 per cent. Roger Federer, arguably one of the greatest tennis players to have ever lived only won 54 per cent of the points he played. Lewis Hamilton has won 35 per cent of the races he has driven. But do we think of them as failures? No, of course not. Because they won when it mattered. But here's the trick – to win when it matters, you have to keep trying. Which means losing sometimes. The only way you definitely fail is if you don't try, or you give up at the first sign of adversity.

A key idea for turning adversity into an asset is this magic trick: any adversity you face, imagine that's the paragraph in your biography before the success comes. Then write the next paragraph. What would be the sweetest turnaround you can think of? What would be the most satisfying end to your movie? That's what you need to make happen. That way, when the challenges come, and they definitely will, you don't need to throw in the towel or pivot to a whole new goal. You just need to keep on moving, and trust that persistence will get you to the finish line. And when you finally make it? After all the struggles and setbacks? That victory will taste so much sweeter because of the fight it took to get there.

Stan Lee created his first hit comic when he was just shy of his thirty-ninth birthday. Henry Ford was forty-five when he launched the Model T. Ray Kroc was fifty-two when he bought McDonald's. I was twenty-four years old when I threw the punch that landed me in prison for the third time in my life. It sounds like a dead-end moment, but inside those prison walls I finally found the help I needed. I started my journey of rehabilitation and laid the foundations for the life I live today. That so-called wrong decision? It became the turning point that allowed me to be where I am now.

Life's twists and turns don't fit neatly into the boxes of 'right' and 'wrong'. Decisions that seem disastrous in the moment can sometimes lead to opportunities we couldn't have imagined. And let's be real about this idea of the 'perfect decision'. It doesn't exist. You could make what feels like the most logical, flawless choice today, only to have the world turned upside down tomorrow by AI robots, a pandemic or World War 3.

Life is messy, unpredictable and constantly shifting – and so are we. Our values, goals and circumstances evolve, which means today's right could be tomorrow's wrong. The truth? Every decision you make is a mix of hope and calculated risk, and its value isn't clear until you fully lean into it and see where it takes you.

Failure isn't the enemy. Not trying is. Obstacles are lessons. The only possible failure is if the story stops before success happens, and the beauty of that is you're 100 per cent in control of whether you stop or not – so what is there to fear if you're in complete control? You have the power to never stop writing your story. Every sentence is the next opportunity for that satisfying win to come. Which means those butterflies in your stomach don't have to be the butterflies of fear. You can simply choose to interpret them as butterflies of excitement ahead of your inevitable success. Whether it's now, the next time, or ten times from now, it's waiting for you to reach it.

Changing How You See Failure

Here's an exercise to change how you see failure and recognize its role in your progress. Grab yourself a notebook and recount a recent setback. Write about what went wrong and be honest with yourself – no excuses, no sugar-coating. Now, dig a little deeper. What has this experience taught you? How has it equipped you with new skills or insights? Next, ask yourself: *How has this moved me closer to my goals?* You may have even learned something new about your goals. Then try to list the practical things you can do differently based on what you've learned, and focus on how doing those things are going to get you to your goals.

Now, you've written an action plan. And suddenly that setback isn't a setback. It's a small detour on the ultimate journey to where you want to get to.

Next create a mantra based on what you have learned from these previous setbacks about how you will approach whatever comes next. Write down a simple affirmation to remind yourself that there's no such thing as a right or wrong decision – only the opportunity to learn, adapt and grow. Here are some examples to get you started: 'I trust myself to navigate whatever comes next', 'Every choice is a chance to grow', 'I have the strength to make any situation work for me', 'There's no wrong choice – only the one I commit to'. The next time you face a decision, take a moment and repeat your mantra to yourself. This will remind you that you are capable of adapting to whatever comes your way – and help you take action without overthinking. Repeat your mantra often, and watch as decision-making becomes less about fear and more about growth.

Time is Fleeting

Life is fleeting. The world doesn't care about our little dramas or daily routines. It was spinning aeons before us and will keep spinning aeons after. Even the biggest legends eventually fade.

Think about it: do you remember your great-great-grandparents? Their struggles? Their triumphs? Probably not. And in 120 years or so, everyone that is currently alive on the planet will be gone. When we think on this scale, it's easy to be fearful or to think that we're a failure, having no impact in the long run. But that's the wrong way of looking at it. Let's face it: we're a blip on the cosmic radar, yet we waste so much of this precious time we have worrying about things that, in the grand scheme of things, mean nothing. Stuck in a soul-sucking job? Holding back because you're scared of what people will say? Here's a reality check . . . Their opinions? Meaningless. Their judgement? Forgotten faster than the next TikTok trend. Against the backdrop of infinity, none of it matters. What does matter is how you choose to spend your time here. Because you don't get a replay. Life isn't a Netflix series you can binge and restart. It's one go, one shot. So why waste it holding back?

Ever notice how fast a seven-day holiday flies by? You blink and are back at your desk, dreaming of the beach you just stepped off. Life is like that too, only there's no next year's holiday waiting. This is it. When it's over, it's over. The question is, are you living in a way that makes your time here feel worth it?

Try this: draw seventy-eight squares on a piece of paper, each representing a year of life. Cross out the ones you've already lived. Look at what's left. Feels like less than you thought, doesn't it? Yet so many people live like they've got all the time in the world, zoning out on their phones, staying in dead-end jobs or holding on to toxic relationships. They put off their dreams, thinking they'll get to them later. Newsflash: 'later' isn't guaranteed. Every second you spend waiting is a second you'll never get back.

So, it's time to create a life that feels like a perpetual holiday. When all is said and done, you'll want to sit back, nod to yourself and sport a proud smile. Why? Because you'll know that your brief flicker of time on this earth was not merely spent but spent wisely.

See Hate as Insanity

A big fear that keeps many people stuck, and I mean a lot of people, is the fear of what other people will say or think about them. Imagine a worst-case scenario – an online troll or hater! That is most people's worst nightmare.

I remember my first hater, and they were the last one that ever really affected me after I realized one important thing! When my business was just taking off, I was at a book-writing club in Portsmouth, buzzing over an e-book I'd recently written. My business coach, a sound voice of reason in my life at the time, had just praised it to the high heavens. 'Mate, that's some incredible stuff in there. Ever thought of writing a book?' With those words, my ambition took flight. As I discussed my e-book at the book club, in the heat of the moment, a fellow attendee at that writers' club asked to read it. Naturally, I agreed. But then, what began as a single email address written on a piece of paper morphed into a chain of them, when it was passed around like a secret note in class. So, I shot off my e-book to everyone who put their email down. The response? While most were silent, one bloke took it upon himself to send me a meticulously crafted hate-mail. This wasn't just any rant; this was a full-blown Shakespearean soliloquy. Words that might have won literary prizes elsewhere now served as daggers, tearing into me. 'Snake oil . . . Your dad would be ashamed,' he wrote, every line dripping with disdain. About to lose my temper and do something stupid, I turned to my coach. Should I face this hater head-on at the next meeting? Draft a counterargument? Or simply hit delete and forget this ever happened?

My coach's advice was pure gold. He painted a vivid picture: 'Imagine you're in a psychiatric ward. A person with severe psychosis hurls insults at you. Would you take it to heart?' My answer? Of course not. You see, these people, like that Shakespearean hater, are battling their own demons. Their hatred? It's about them, not me. The initial sting of such hatred was sharp, but with time, the pain dulled. Not because the hate stopped (just glance at the comments on my Facebook ads), but because I learned to see it for what it was: noise. Accusations of scams or running a cult? Water off a duck's back. Especially as success came knocking. I realized I had less and less to prove to these strangers. Their opinions? Merely reflections of their own insecurities and personal battles.

Go and look at any of the greatest films, books, computer games or products of all time. There will be one-star reviews. *The Godfather*? Crap, mate. *War and Peace*? Bit long. We live in a world where everyone's voice can be heard – and for a variety of reasons, some people get something out of being negative. But that's their problem. What if you reframe it and imagine for a moment what it must be like to feel relentlessly negative about everything? What a sad, empty, colourless life that must be. You'd probably feel sorry for someone like that. You certainly wouldn't ask them for advice. So why should you listen to their opinion on something you've done? Don't give haters the power to influence your emotions or your journey. Recognize their hurt and empathize from a distance, but never let it deter you. After all, it's just noise amidst the symphony of your success. So, turn up your own volume and drown it out. Because at the end of the day, you know your worth, and no hater can take that away from you.

Ironically, you know the e-book I mentioned? Here's the funny part, or what I like to call a 'universe moment' . . . the exact e-book the hater tore apart and criticized? Not only did it make me stronger and prepare me for any future hate to come, I doubled down on my efforts with it, published it to my website as a free download, and years later it was that exact e-book which an editor from Penguin Random House, the number-one book publisher in the world, read and which landed me this book deal. I realize now that my hater was just jealous and entirely wrong. But the scary part is, imagine if I'd listened to him and deleted the whole thing?

I bet that kind of thing happens all the time. Opportunities missed. Destinies changed. Because of one random hater. So, to the Shakespearean hater, if you ever end up reading this somehow, I won. But I also hope this book helps you, because there is no animosity on my end, you were a part of my journey – so, thank you.

Self-Hate

But what if the biggest hater in your life isn't out there – it's you? You dream about doing something meaningful that really matters to you, but then you shut yourself down. You tell yourself it's selfish and redirect your focus towards someone else: your partner, your kids, your friends, your job. There's this weird stigma around chasing your own goals as if it makes you self-centred. But let's unpack that word: 'selfish'. It's not inherently bad; it simply means prioritizing yourself. And prioritizing yourself doesn't have to mean you're neglecting the people you care about.

You matter, too. Somewhere along the way, most of us learned that being selfless is the gold standard and that putting others first is the only way to be a good person. But sacrificing your own needs doesn't make you better for anyone else. In fact, when you neglect yourself, you're running on empty, and that doesn't help anyone. Investing in yourself isn't just okay, it's necessary. Because when you're happy, fulfilled and thriving, you bring that energy into every relationship and every interaction. You don't just show up for others; you show up *better*.

When you care for your own mental, emotional and physical needs, you build a foundation that benefits everyone around you. So stop hating on yourself – because when you take care of yourself, you show up stronger and more capable for the people who matter most.

Swap Risks for Rewards

A lot of what we are discussing here involves risk, and people hate risk, so let's break that down! In fact, let's flip it on its head. Taking risks is an incredible aspect of life. It's time to change our perspective and stop fearing and avoiding them. Since childhood, we've been conditioned to view risks negatively. Rarely would you hear a parent say, 'Have a great day at school and don't forget to take plenty of risks, Jenny.' And when people discourage you from taking risks, they may seem well-meaning, but their motivations can be selfish. Their fear of you getting hurt or upset drives them to persuade you to play it safe. But what they fail to realize is that they're depriving you of the rewards that come from taking risks.

If you find risks frightening, imagine how much more daunting it would be to live with regrets. Regret is a haunting feeling – knowing you didn't take a chance when you had the opportunity. If we take a risk, sure, we might fail. But we need to balance that against the potential future regret if we don't even try. The problem is when you let the fear of taking risks run all areas of your life. Because there's one zone that none of us wants to be in.

The Comfort Zone

It sounds nice, right? Who doesn't love comfort? Especially a whole zone of it! Sounds amazing. But the problem is it's a dead zone. Nothing can grow there. A paradox of life is that the one place we will definitely not build the resilience to create actual true material comfort in our lives is the comfort zone. Mark Manson, the author of the 20-million-copy bestseller *The Subtle Art of Not Giving a F*ck*, has a chapter in the book about how essential suffering is and how important the meaning we give it is. Not only is suffering a permanent fact of life – if you think about it, so many of the most important things in life are also hard. In many ways, their importance is bound up in how hard they are.

Why is running a marathon impressive? Because we know the challenges that have been met and overcome to achieve it. It is through struggling against challenges that we create meaning. It's why a *Rocky* film isn't just Rocky easily defeating a succession of boxers who aren't as good as him. It's in overcoming our greatest challenges that we learn. This doesn't mean that we should go around sitting on drawing pins just for the sake of it. But if there was a world without discomfort, we wouldn't know what true comfort felt like when we actually experienced it.

Discomfort, fear, failure and risks are not going anywhere, and time is waiting for nobody. But they don't have to control you. They don't have to stop you from living the life you want. When you understand these factors, face them, and take action despite them, they start to become powerless to negatively influence you.

Fear is a type of adversity that will always walk beside us. But when you stop running from it, when you stare it down and dissect it, something shifts. You take back control. You stop being a passenger in your own life. And fear, strangely, starts working in your favour. Not because it disappears, but because you move with it, learn from it and transform it into something that helps you. And when you can do that, the excuses fade, the hesitation quiets, and what's left is just the next step closer to where you want to be.

Key Takeaways

- Fear is a very old and powerful part of being a human. It is there for a very good reason, but our fight-or-flight system is too sensitive and gets set off when it shouldn't.
- Learn to differentiate between real fear and fake fear. Look a situation that feels scary in the face and ask yourself: *What's the worst thing that could happen?*
- Reframe failure. Every person who has achieved anything in this world, failed to begin with.
- The only guarantee of permanent failure is never trying. Failure is temporary, as long as you keep on trying again.
- See haters as expressing an issue in themselves, not you. Their negativity is their problem.
- Risk isn't the enemy – regret is. Playing it safe comes at a cost. Taking risks may feel scary, but the real danger is looking back and realizing you didn't reap any rewards.
- Beware of your comfort zone. Learn to embrace everyday discomfort – it's the price we pay for getting things done.

As we've seen, some of our biggest fears are rooted in the need for acceptance, approval and not wanting to be judged. It's wired into us. We don't want to be cast out, rejected, laughed at. So we hold back. We edit ourselves. We become who we think we need to be, just to stay safe or be liked. But that safety comes at a cost. The more you shape-shift to fit into other people's expectations, the further you drift from who you actually are. And let me tell you from experience, the hardest thing you will ever do isn't building a business or changing your life – it's having the courage to be fully, unapologetically yourself in a world that's constantly trying to mould you into something else.

The next chapter is about finding the courage to be radically authentic. To stop performing. To drop the mask. To be seen as you really are – not just accepted, but self-approved. Because real freedom doesn't come from being liked by everyone. It comes from knowing you're living in alignment with who you really are.

CHAPTER 5

Radical Authenticity

'Oh *him*. My mate told me stories about him from when he was growing up. He's a proper psycho.'

I am sat in a toilet cubicle during Fire Up, my motivational speaking event, and two strangers are talking about my event that has just finished. At first, I am enjoying that they are talking about me at all. But then one of them makes that throwaway remark. Suddenly I am dragged back into my past.

I am the man who made his best friend cry because I wouldn't stop punching someone we'd got into a fight with. He was trying to drag me away, crying and shouting my name: 'Lewis, stop it. Stop it, Lewis!' But I couldn't switch the anger off because it was all that I had. Every punch thrown was an attempt to feel like I mattered. I am the eighteen-year-old teenager who went to his pre-sentence report meeting, where the probation service makes a recommendation to the judge for appropriate sentencing.

It's known in the criminal community to be on your best behaviour during this meeting. My lawyer had told me that I was probably looking at a minimum of eight years in prison. That day, I turned up late, crossed my arms, and gave the probation officer an intimidating look as if to say, 'Do your worst.' I remember her being shocked when she asked me questions like 'Do you not care you're going to prison for a long time?' and I would say 'No'. Or 'Do you realize the impact you've had on your victims and their families?' and I answered 'No'. Was this because I wanted to appear tough or mask some underlying emotion? It didn't seem that way, at least. The honest truth is I didn't know how to feel. I didn't know what empathy and remorse were, let alone have a chance to feel or understand them. The darkness in my life had caused me to completely shut down.

The probation officer sent me for a psychiatric assessment to go with my pre-sentence report. I didn't think anything of it and just saw it as another appointment, along with everything else that comes with being in the system. I turned up at a mental health facility and met with Dr Sadler. He asked me very normal questions; nothing stood out to me.

When the report came back, I was expecting it to say I was just a bad lad but essentially normal. But that's when I had that transformative moment of being diagnosed with Antisocial Personality Disorder, along with Borderline Personality Disorder (called Emotionally Unstable Personality Disorder at the time) and Bipolar Type 2. I went straight to Google, typed it all in, and within seconds the word 'psychopath' was all over my screen.

When I read the report generated from this meeting, I saw that it had told the judge that I would kill someone one day and that I was recommended for an IPP, an Indefinite Public Protection order, meaning I would be sentenced to prison and not allowed out until I was deemed safe to be released back into society.

When I was sat in that cubicle at Fire Up, it suddenly seemed like everything that I had accomplished no longer mattered. This, despite the fact I had just come back from three months's travelling in Thailand, Cambodia, Singapore and Malaysia and finally experienced true freedom for the first time in my life. I had kept doing my coaching sessions via video calls with clients the whole time, and to my surprise they were just as effective. Before long, I was coaching people from all over the world, online, from wherever I wanted. I had returned to the UK after travelling abroad, determined to start university. But it didn't take long to see it wasn't for me. The knowledge I'd found online and applied in my business was miles ahead of anything I was being taught in a classroom. By then, I'd already built a six-figure business and I was crafting my own strategies to scale it up. It became clear that I didn't need a classroom just yet to keep climbing.

So, I had thrown myself entirely into my business, devoured every piece of content I could find, enrolled in training courses, and worked with coaches and mentors. With clients already onboard and real momentum building, I decided it was time to revisit my dream of creating a community – this time online.

The clients were pouring in. Other coaches were contacting me, asking how this new young coach was getting the incredible results that I was. They couldn't wrap their heads around how I was landing so many clients and making such strides. But when I laid out my game plan, their reaction was always 'Ah, that makes sense. Never looked at it that way before.' This was a bit of a turning point, where I began to realize that maybe I wasn't the dunce I always thought I was. I seemed to have a knack for cracking things open in ways others couldn't.

But despite all that success, that overheard comment hit upon a vulnerability. Something I had been working on. Accepting who I was – my flaws, my past. But in that exact moment, when I wanted to be concentrating entirely on what I was doing so well, the spotlight was on my past and the things I didn't do the same way as other people. It made me think of how, back in the thick of my therapy inside rehab, I had found myself clicking with one of the counsellors, Lisa. She'd prodded me to talk about my dad, a subject I'd avoided like the plague my whole life. She kept telling me it was alright and that I could trust her. Then I completely lost it. Before I knew it, I was shrieking, 'Why was he so horrible to me?' It was as if I wasn't even in control; words just started tumbling out of my mouth. 'Why didn't he love me?' That moment was key to me finding what was at the heart of so much of my life up until that point. I realized that I had yet to truly open up, and start to understand how being vulnerable could become one of my biggest superpowers.

The Strength to be Vulnerable

In a world that often equates strength with self-reliance, being vulnerable can feel almost impossible. It's like you need to be your own unconquerable castle. But real strength isn't about putting up walls; it's about tearing them down. Vulnerability is your hidden superpower – the raw force that fuels true personal growth and lets you live authentically. You've probably spent your whole life trying to fit in. But true authenticity is about embracing who you truly are because, at the end of the day, if you're not living for yourself, you're not really living at all. Vulnerability is not weakness; it's the courage to show up and be seen, however people respond. It's about being honest with yourself and others about your fears and desires.

Integrating vulnerability into your daily life begins by sharing your feelings with friends or family members. This might mean simply telling them when you're scared, or being honest about your dreams and aspirations, or acknowledging when you need help. Notice how it feels to open up, and how doing so affects your relationships. Be kind to yourself when you feel vulnerable. Recognize that vulnerability is a sign of courage. When we embrace our vulnerabilities, we allow ourselves to be truly seen, fostering deeper connections with others and building genuine relationships.

Mutual vulnerability is key to so much of therapy and AA and NA meetings. It only works because the sharing of struggles opens a connection with others. I have seen, time and time again, how once you stop putting on that brave face and pretending everything's fine when inside you're struggling – and instead you share your struggle – people feel able to be their real, vulnerable self back.

Why did that word 'psycho' echo so loud for me? Because it carried with it all the force of that word, 'buffoon', spoken so many years before. Because it was the crystallization of everything that I couldn't do in the same way as other people. That word, that no doctor would ever use, was the lurid popular label for the bundle of disorders and conditions that I had. It said that it didn't matter what actions I took, because underneath it all I was wired differently to other people. That I was somehow just wrong. But then I came to a realization. The fact this word had landed the way it did meant I needed to stay with it. Not ignore it, bury my head in the sand and try to pretend it had nothing to do with me. I had to practise radical authenticity.

What did they even mean by 'psycho'? They probably had a Hannibal Lecter–type serial killer in their head. Someone who feels no emotions. Someone manipulative and devious who is capable of terrible things. I imagined the worst version of that word. Then I stood next to it and compared myself to it. Had I been capable of things that most people would describe as terrible? Yes, that was undeniable; I couldn't ignore my past. Did I process all of my emotions in exactly the same way as a neurotypical person? Definitely not. But did that mean that I was without feelings? Here it got complicated.

There has been a lot of research into conditions like mine

that suggests that we actually don't *feel* certain feelings, and instead we rely on *cognitive empathy* where the brain processes our emotions intellectually. This means people like me might not feel what you're feeling, but we can understand it and respond just as deeply. It's just different. We might not shed a tear during a sad movie, but we're perfectly capable of making rational, empathetic decisions that benefit others. We are capable of great acts of kindness. The exact wiring might be different, but the outcomes don't have to be.

Then I started thinking properly about all the other features of those who are popularly called 'psychopaths'. We tend to lack fear. We are confident. We are emotionally detached. We are persuasive. We are goal-oriented. We thrive under stress. We have huge amounts of energy and need to constantly be stimulated. Now, of course, any of those characteristics taken to extremes, or without balance, could be a bad thing. But suddenly that list sounded to me like it was describing a surgeon, or a CEO, or a general.

After a lot of honest work with myself, I got to a place where I'd opened a window and let light in on what felt like the worst thing about me – this horrible dark locked room at the centre of me. I was even grateful for it. The first twenty-five years of my life, I'd let it consume me – and no surprise, that hadn't gone well. But I realized that the last few years I had gone the opposite way and been suppressing it. The real breakthrough came when I stopped resisting it and started integrating. As Carl Jung famously said, 'One does not become enlightened by imagining figures of light, but by making the darkness conscious.' I know it's quite a philosophical mouthful, but it means you can't have light without darkness because they define each other. Without shadows, we wouldn't understand what light is.

The odds are that you've not been labelled a psychopath. But our wider understanding of non-neurotypicality is transforming our understanding of strengths and weaknesses.

The New Normal

When I was growing up, there was normal and anything else was pretty much bad. If you didn't learn best by sitting in a class while a teacher talked at you, you were slow. If you needed more thought and effort put into keeping your attention, you were naughty. If you had trouble regulating your emotions, you were a little thug. If you needed help following sequences of instructions or managing your time, you were lazy. If you found social interaction difficult, you were too shy and needed to get over it.

But, as a society, we are learning that this obsession with 'normal' leaves behind so much. The incredible ability to hyperfocus on detail and use pattern recognition that individuals with Autistic Spectrum Disorder and ADHD often display are superpowers in the right roles and jobs. Non-neurotypical people often literally see the world differently, and because of this they can approach problems from a different angle, or with a completely different framing. And if you want to find a group of people more used to putting in the hard work and staying outside their comfort zone, you'd be hard pressed to find them. So much that the neurotypical find easy, we have had to find entirely new strategies and responses to cope with. Every day, we take ourselves out of our comfort zone and we have the psychological muscles to prove it. We adapt, we show world-class resilience and we thrive.

The key thing to remember, NT (neurotypical) or NNT (non-neurotypical), is that everything is on a spectrum. We have just decided, often quite arbitrarily, that some parts of the spectrum are 'normal' and some aren't. To take one example at random, people with Antisocial Personality Disorder can often blame others for problems in their lives. I'm sure we all know plenty of people (and as we've explored, maybe even ourselves) who that is true of who haven't been diagnosed with or even have a personality disorder. We all have various parts of our personalities that may not seem positive and can overshadow our light. However, some of these traits are there for a reason, and may serve to protect us or provide unique benefits.

We can explore these aspects of ourselves through something that originated with Carl Jung, called 'shadow work'. It's a complex part of psychology – but a very simple version is that we all have parts of ourselves that we don't consciously identify with. These could be fears, emotions, desires or traits that are undesirable, and so we suppress them. However, as we all know, repressing something doesn't make it go away. Our repressed shadow ends up distorting our lives. It is only by finding a way to integrate these aspects of ourselves that we can truly know ourselves and live our lives with radical authenticity. Once we find a way of integrating them into our personality, they become a source of strength, not shame.

It's Not New, It's Just Being Named

It can be tempting to view neurodiversity as something that's been 'invented' recently. But of course it's always been here. What we now call ADHD, autism, dyslexia or sensory processing differences – those things have always been part of the human experience. Neurodiversity is not a TikTok trend or a fashionable diagnosis; it's something that's existed for ever – only now it has a name. But for thousands of years, people who thought differently weren't seen as wired uniquely; they were thought to be broken. And if, against all odds, someone like that managed to make something of themselves? They were called a genius. Some of the most influential people in history would, by today's standards, almost certainly be considered neurodivergent, and because they were somehow able to break through every barrier put in their way, we celebrate them.

But those individuals were few and far between. The majority of neurodiverse people, for the majority of human history, were just left behind. Their lives were a constant battle to fit in, and they had to expend all their energy trying to force themselves to exist in a way that wasn't inherently natural for them. Some of them were medicated, some institutionalized. Even today, in the UK, almost 50 per cent of the prison population is neurodivergent, which is more than three times the percentage in the general population. I speak from personal experience when I say that being in a prison is to see the sharp end of this issue every day.

If we talk the talk of valuing neurodiversity, then we have to walk the walk of it. Because awareness is only the first step. The bigger challenge is to flip the script entirely and stop seeing these traits as problems to be solved and start seeing them as different ways of being. Because in the right environment these 'disorders' can be brought into order. Some of the people who feel the most broken are actually sitting on untapped brilliance.

And when I say 'some', it's probably a lot more than we think. The Chartered Institute of Personnel and Development estimates that as much as 20 per cent of the global population may have ADHD, autism, dyslexia or other cognitive differences, though the majority of them will be undiagnosed. That's one in five – a big chunk of the people around us. But our schools are still run according to old-fashioned rules. Sit down, pay attention, read what's written on the board. If you can't do that, you're not good at school.

There's an old saying, 'If you judge a fish by its ability to climb a tree, it will live its whole life believing it's stupid.' I was that fish my whole young life. Looking up at the tree and thinking I was stupid for not being able to grab even the first branch. But put me in the water and suddenly everything changed. We need to get to a place where we have earlier and more accurate assessments in schools. We need workplaces that are designed for neurodiversity, not just grudgingly accommodate it. And we need to learn to see that different isn't something to shunt to the edges but to put front and centre. When one in five people process the world differently, they're an important missing part of the conversation. The future doesn't belong to the most obedient. It belongs to the most adaptable. And to be truly unlimited, we must start recognizing genius in all its forms – in ourselves, in our colleagues, and in every part of humanity, especially those we've been ignoring the longest.

A Trick of the Mind

The first thing to realize is that pretty much every negative trait can be a positive one in a certain context or seen from a certain angle. As the famous line spoken by Hamlet puts it, 'There is nothing either good or bad, but thinking makes it so.'

Aggression has historically been pretty handy if you were a warrior defending your community. Most of the greatest leaders in human history would be labelled narcissistic these days. Everywhere we look, from the utterly necessary ability to switch off empathy for the suffering of the patient who the surgeon is operating on, to the utter strategic focus of our most admired business leaders, there are people displaying 'negative' traits.

Manipulativeness might sound negative, but when reframed as a persuasive influence, it's a key trait for effective leadership. Great leaders like Steve Jobs use their persuasive abilities to inspire teams and achieve game-changing innovations. Strategic thinking, which could be about outplaying competitors or getting a better deal, could be linked with deceitfulness; however, in the competitive business world, thinking a few steps ahead is crucial and helps with finding innovative solutions that others might overlook, leading to success through smart, calculated moves. Impulsivity, while risky, can also translate to bold, quick decision-making; entrepreneurs like Richard Branson have built empires by seizing opportunities as they arise. And what might seem like irresponsibility is often a willingness to challenge the status quo. Visionaries often take significant risks to push the boundaries of technology and innovation, leading to building crazy things like robots and spaceships!

Even a disregard for norms can drive disruptive innovation. Companies like Uber and Airbnb have revolutionized their industries by challenging existing rules, creating entirely new markets, and transforming the way we live. Grandiosity, or an inflated sense of self, can drive visionary leadership. Figures like Jeff Bezos have inspired entire industries with their huge visions, which people once laughed at and called corporate arrogance. A belief in a future that others can't see has motivated countless people to help turn those visions into reality. Emotional detachment can sometimes be helpful in high-stakes situations. It's a huge advantage to stay calm without being overwhelmed by fear or guilt in certain professions. This doesn't need to be seen as being careless, but about being strategically thoughtful and making decisions grounded in logic rather than emotion.

But what about traits that don't feel like they can be used productively? Maybe you're angry or jealous and can't find a place to fit these feelings into something beneficial for you or others. This is where you can use your shadows to identify signals. Sometimes it's our shadows that point us to what is deeper, which can help us understand ourselves better and continue working towards a complete version of ourselves. It's like the mental smokescreens and triggers I was talking about earlier – but these are a bit deeper; they feel ingrained and almost part of your personality, as they have been there for as long as you can remember.

In modern life, anger is often stigmatized. We're told to 'stay calm' and 'be nice', even when someone else is in the wrong. But anger isn't always inherently negative. It's a biological signal, alerting us that something or someone is threatening our well-being, safety or values. Sure, we could slap on a smile and suppress and ignore that anger, pushing it further into our subconscious, but what does that do? It suppresses a natural emotion, violates our values, and doesn't allow us to handle the real situation.

Imagine you're at work, and a colleague keeps dumping their tasks on you, assuming you'll take care of everything. You feel a simmering anger but push it aside, thinking, *I don't want to be difficult*. Over time, that anger grows, manifesting as resentment or burnout – or worse, it spills out into other areas of your life, and you start acting like a pushover with other people, too.

Instead of ignoring the anger, what if you listened to it? Anger is telling you that your boundaries are being violated. By recognizing this signal, you can take action – perhaps by having a conversation to clarify roles or saying no to additional responsibilities. In this way, anger becomes a protector of your time, energy and self-respect. Anger, if provoked by injustice and used as a fuel, can be a force for positive transformation. It's what gave women the vote and ended the transatlantic slave trade.

Guilt can feel very oppressive too. People treat it like a cloud hanging over their heads, forcing them down and making them feel crap. But what if guilt isn't here to punish you? What if it is just pointing you back towards what matters when you've gone off track? Picture this: a friend invites you to a party, but you've had an absolute nightmare of a week. You cancel at the last minute and throw out a little white lie about being unwell. But then, later on, that guilt creeps in.

At this point, you could wallow in it, or you could ask yourself: *What's this really about?* Maybe it's telling you that honesty matters to you. Maybe it's about showing up for the people who show up for you. Next time, instead of the white lie, you say, 'I'm shattered tonight, but I appreciate the invite.' Guilt, when you listen to it, isn't trying to make you feel small; instead, it can be a gentle reminder of your values. It can be your nudge to get back in line with who you really are.

Jealousy is that nasty little twinge we hate to admit we feel, especially when scrolling through someone else's highlight reel online. They're making more money, they're with the perfect partner, they have the perfect abs – and suddenly you're stuck thinking, *Why not me?* The go-to response? Shove it down, pretend it's not there, or worse, bitch about them or leave a snarky comment. But what if jealousy is actually trying to tell you something important? What if it's a sign that this is what you want too? Instead of letting it eat away at you, stop and ask: *What's this really about?* Maybe their success isn't triggering envy. It could merely be shining a light on something you want in your own life. Jealousy doesn't have to be a weakness; it can be clarity. It's your subconscious saying, 'Hey, this matters to you, go after it.'

When you stop seeing your shadows as enemies and start treating them as signals, you unlock a deeper level of self-awareness. Anger, guilt, jealousy – these emotions might feel uncomfortable, even shameful, but they're not random. They're trying to tell you something about what you value, what you need or where you're out of alignment. The more you lean into these signals, the more you'll understand yourself – and the better equipped you'll be to handle life's challenges. Shadows don't exist to hold you back; they exist to guide you towards a stronger, more complete version of yourself. So, instead of fighting them, start listening to them. The key is understanding and integrating them ethically. This is where self-awareness comes into play. Our shadows don't need to be suppressed or demonized. Instead, they should be recognized, understood, and channelled constructively. When we own these shadows within ourselves, we can use them to our advantage without letting them control us.

Spot Your Shadows

The first step in shadow work is spotting when your shadow self is at play. Get brutally honest with yourself, with no judgement or shame. What are the times when you have been ashamed about how you've behaved? Ask yourself: *What was really going on? What was I truly feeling?* Write it all down. When you see your shadow clearly, it stops lurking in the corners of your mind. To begin with, you'll justify your behaviour to yourself. You'll find reasons why it wasn't your fault, but push on past that and get to the negative trait at the heart of it.

Then, flip the script. For every 'negative' trait you uncover, try to identify its hidden strength. Is your stubbornness really determination in disguise? Could your impulsivity be reframed as bold decision-making? Get curious and playful with this. Next time you notice a shadow trait emerging, pause and ask: *How can I use this trait constructively now?*

Once you've identified and reframed your shadow, it's time to embrace it. Visualize a safe space and imagine your shadow self walking in. This might be an angry version of you, a scared child or something entirely unexpected. Have a conversation. Ask it: *Why are you here? What do you need from me? How can we work together? How can we channel this energy to benefit us or others?* This isn't about fixing or silencing your shadow, but understanding it. Thank it for trying to protect you and for the gifts it provides, and let it know you're ready to work together.

Balancing your shadows is crucial. I'm in no way advocating for a life without emotion or empathy. Rather, it's about recognizing that there are times when these 'dark' traits can be incredibly beneficial. What people call 'dark' traits can be positive tools in the right hands. It's all about how you use them. If you ask my business partners, my clients or my team – they'd all tell you I'm different. But that difference? That's what gives me my edge. Like the other successful entrepreneurs I've mentioned, I have this ability to take risks that would completely paralyse most people. Fear doesn't hit me in the same way; I make tough decisions quickly, always focusing on the bigger picture rather than getting lost in the noise of the moment. And yeah, I'll admit it – I've got a streak of arrogance. I've always believed I can do things better than some, and that confidence has driven me to take on challenges most people wouldn't even go near. These traits have not just been helpful to my success, but absolutely essential to it. They've allowed me to stay calm under pressure, make bold moves, and helped me push through situations that make others hesitate and overthink. I've made hundreds of decisions where everyone around me was scratching their heads, not understanding what I was doing. And when it comes to my clients, these same qualities take on a different shape. While many people get swept up in their clients' emotions, paralysed by the fear of saying the wrong thing, I cut straight through the noise. It's sometimes uncomfortable, but it's always what's needed to break ingrained patterns and move forward.

Let me share an example. One of my clients – we'll call him David – was running a small business on the edge of collapse. The company couldn't survive much longer unless drastic action was taken. The problem? One staff member. This person had been with him since day one but their poor performance and negativity were dragging the whole team down. David knew it, but whenever we discussed it, he'd say, 'I can't fire him, he's like family, I'd feel awful.' Week after week, he avoided the conversation, hoping things would somehow fix themselves, but every week, the business was bleeding out and getting closer and closer to the point of no return.

I didn't sugar-coat it. I told him straight: 'David, do you want to sacrifice your entire business, your other employees, and everything you've built just to avoid feeling guilty for one person?' Then we worked through a plan for the conversation they needed to have. It was one of the hardest things he'd ever done, but he made the call. And the impact was immediate. The team's morale improved, and the business not only survived but started thriving again. All he'd needed was someone to call him out – but not everybody is prepared to do that.

Now let me tell you about another client, a woman we'll call Sarah. Sarah had been stuck in the same loop for years, replaying a trauma that had left her life in pieces. A messy break-up and friends and family taking sides. But the real issue wasn't the past any more; it was Sarah's refusal to let go of the victim narrative that she was playing on repeat. She told the story so often that it became her identity. Every time I asked her what she wanted for her future, she would circle back to the pain of her past. To make matters worse, her friends and family were enabling her, constantly agreeing that she'd been wronged and validating how she felt. But this only works up to a point, and I knew we couldn't continue letting it play out for ever. I had to be direct. So I told Sarah, 'The only person still suffering is you. You have to decide – do you want to keep being the victim, or do you want to take control of your life?' It hit her like a ton of bricks. For the first time, she realized that holding on to the pain wasn't protecting her any more but imprisoning her. Together, we worked on reframing her narrative. She started making choices for herself instead of reacting to her past, and over time she transformed into someone who wasn't defined by her trauma but by the strength she'd found in overcoming it.

That's what I do. I don't sweet-talk my clients or tiptoe around the hard stuff. I give them the truth they need to hear so they can move forward, break free from the stories that hold them back, and create the life they want to live. Because sometimes the biggest breakthroughs come from the toughest conversations. The point here isn't that my traits are some golden ticket – they're not. Being me comes with enormous challenges, there's no doubt about it. But by reframing my shadows as a positive, I have been able to find a way to integrate those parts of myself into a whole that benefits me and others.

This isn't just limited to qualities relating to those who are labelled psychopaths, there are all sorts of non-neurotypical behaviours that we can all learn from. That 'impulsivity' or 'inattentiveness' that individuals with ADHD 'suffer' from? Well, that often goes hand in hand with creativity and dynamism. Dyslexia, which is often understood as a learning difficulty, often means that dyslexics are brilliant at solving problems and being creative. Just as we understand the need for biodiversity on our planet, we need diversity of human experience. We need to start seeing neurological quirks as potential superpowers.

When you reframe these differences, you realize they're not something to be ashamed of. So-called disorders can bring something powerful to the table – whether it's a fresh perspective, a unique talent, or an ability to connect the dots in ways others simply can't. The brain is a complex, beautifully messy organ that doesn't need to fit into society's narrow definition of 'normal'. You can embrace your quirks and your edges and understand that these differences aren't just parts of you – they *are* you. And they might just be the key to unlocking your full potential. Because once you start loving that neurodivergent edge, you stop fighting who you are and start using who you are.

Rule Breaking

One of the biggest parts of myself I have learned to use constructively is my natural urge to transgress boundaries. For the first twenty-five years of my life, if I saw a rule, I had to break it. It was a complete compulsion. The idea that you should listen to teachers, lawyers, police officers – it just felt so pointless. Now, of course, I know that this is a big symptom of Antisocial Personality Disorder. And while I have definitely got better at following certain rules, my instinct on being shown a rule is always going to be to ask why. This is especially true for so many of those unspoken, unenforced rules that we have all internalized as ones we have to follow. You know – the ones about getting a job with a company, working hard, rising up through the ranks, buying a house and settling down to have a family. These aren't laws that anyone enforces, but are rules that a great many people live by as if they're law. But what happens if that path doesn't make you happy? What if you want a different shape of life? What if you don't want to own property, to be tied to one job? What if you want the freedom of a digital nomad, working wherever you can plug your laptop in? So often, anyone who wants something different from the status quo is made to feel like they are the ones in the wrong. But who decided that was the 'right' way to live?

I'm not saying break every rule. Don't start only crossing the road when the little man is red. Remember that so many of the things that shape what we believe is possible are rules that don't exist anywhere apart from our minds. But they still have such an impact on how we behave: how we dress, who we love and how, where we live . . . And that classic unspoken rule from within the world of work that is such a source of friction: should you stay late if you care about your job?

Generation Clash

The generation known as Baby Boomers – that is, those born between 1946 and 1964 – grew up believing that working long hours is how you demonstrate your commitment and dedication, and how you earn success. They saw fifty-plus-hour weeks as normal, and were used to starting before 9 a.m. and finishing after 7 p.m., putting their work life above their home life. By the time the next generation – Generation X (born between 1965 and 1980) – came along, they were starting to want a better work–life balance, but the vast majority of them still worked more hours than they were paid for. Then Millennials (born between 1981 and 1996) took things a step further and looked for more flexibility and a better work–life balance. And now Gen Z (born between 1997 and 2012) value freedom, purpose and meaning. They would rather protect their mental wellbeing than chase that promotion. They often prefer non-traditional work schedules.

To someone stuck in the Baby Boomer mindset, a Gen Z worker may appear lazy because the way that they work is so different. To a Gen Z, the idea that someone would work sixty-hour weeks in a job they don't enjoy and risk their mental wellbeing feels obviously wrong. So often I hear about clashes between people who have internalized different sets of rules about what trying hard at work looks like. Young colleagues are decried as lazy and self-absorbed. Older colleagues are deemed out of step with the modern age.

For 95 per cent of people, their main goal in life is career-focused. Something I say a lot to help people discover if they are on the right path, or just walking along somebody else's path, is to ask themselves: *Would I be happy having the job and life of my boss's boss in exchange for the next ten to fifteen years of my life?* Because mimicking your boss's steps won't work if their destination isn't where you want to get to.

Don't be afraid to stretch beyond a box you feel you've been put in. Life is too short to follow rules that aren't even rules.

Assassinate Conformity

Conformity is a silent assassin that annihilates authenticity. We spend so much time worrying about fitting in that we forget who we actually are. It's like we're all wearing these masks, afraid that if we show our true selves, we'll be judged. But fitting in is over-rated. It's time to own your weirdness and embrace every quirky, unconventional and raw part of yourself. We've been trained to crave acceptance and seek out belonging by blending into the crowd, but in doing so, we dilute the very essence of what makes us unique. We censor ourselves far more harshly than anyone else ever would.

The truth is, the world doesn't need more people who fit in – it needs more people who stand out, people who are unapologetically themselves. So stop apologizing for being different. Stop trying to fit into a mould that was never meant for you. The moment you let go of who you think you should be is the moment you start living as the person you truly are. Own your weird, flaunt it, and let the world catch up with you. Because when you're truly authentic, when you stop giving a damn about fitting in, that's when you unlock your real power.

I have learned to temper my suspicion of all authority, but it means that I always ask whether those in positions of power deserve to be there. It means I cross-examine my heroes and I am hugely rigorous about who I set as my role models. Because my natural inclination is always to ask why. Why are they the people we look up to and admire? What have they actually done?

Something inside me has always seen people as equals, and that the illusion of fear created by hierarchy simply doesn't exist. This could be looked at as immature rebellion or as innate independence. Others obey the establishment and perceived authorities just because they're conditioned to believe it's the only viable path and they're incapable of charting their own course in life. However, it's very important to remember that each individual is driven by their own personal agenda and so you must protect your freedom at all costs – otherwise, others may suffocate your dreams. Imagine being ninety years old and looking back on your fleeting life and realizing you didn't spend your time on earth doing what you wanted because everyone around you pushed you in a different direction.

Here's a reality check: we are all equal human beings born

on this planet, entitled to the same rights as each other. No one holds the right to dictate other people's lives. Though societal norms may make us feel compelled to conform, they're essentially an emotional cage trapping us.

The logic is simple: learn from and follow people who have what you want. Society tells you to ignore 'fake online business gurus' and listen to politicians or business lecturers instead. But take a look at their lives: the cars they drive, their happiness levels, the results they've achieved. Now, look at me. Most would brush off my advice because I'm covered in tattoos and have a criminal past. But that's ignorance that would rob you of real, raw experience that can genuinely help you achieve a life of total freedom.

On the other hand, listening to someone in a suit with a fancy title might seem smart, but their advice could land you in a minimum-wage job, drowning in debt, working until you drop dead. Harsh, but true. Value comes in many forms, and in today's diverse culture, we need to question what success actually looks like. Learn from those who have what you want, not just from those society tells you to follow.

The Power of Resourcefulness

Ever catch yourself thinking, *I just don't have what it takes to succeed*? Maybe you feel you don't have the time, money, energy or experience to progress in life? And perhaps it feels all too easy to just give up? After serving time in prison, I spent another half a year in rehab. During that stretch, I relied on benefits, with my wallet feeling lighter than ever. Once out, my slate seemed empty. No cash or accolades to my name. My days were consumed with learning, nights with working, and weekends attending support meetings. On paper, I had nothing! But buried beneath all the perceived lack was my most potent asset – my mindset. I was motivated to achieve anything I set my mind to; and that's the magic potion.

The first step to unlocking this inner potential is to know that it's there, possible for you to harness, and not to distance yourself from it by comparing yourself to others and thinking it's not within you. I remember looking at successful people and thinking, *I'm nothing like them*. They seemed to possess something I didn't – maybe more intellect, ambition or talent. Their lives seemed impossible for someone like me. I thought that even if I gave it my all, it would never be enough because the truth was, I didn't think I was enough. The moment I challenged this narrative, to acknowledge that perhaps I did have what it took, I started to keep pace with them and sometimes even overtake them. If you've ever felt different, maybe it's time to celebrate that uniqueness. Because those successful figures you admire? Perhaps you don't just have the potential to match them, you have the capacity to outshine them in ways you haven't even envisioned yet.

Your true potential isn't something tangible; it's not material resources, equipment, cash or certificates. It's your intrinsic mental state. It's about tapping into that wellspring of determination and passion. When you embody resourcefulness, suddenly every other resource becomes attainable. So take a look into the mirror and recognize that the most dynamic resource is staring back at you. It's YOU. You're equipped, ready, and more than capable of making a lasting imprint on the world and achieving anything you want.

Think about it. Someone who isn't resourceful might say, 'I don't have the education or the money.' Someone who is resourceful would say, 'I will see what free education I can find and get started and build from there.' So, when challenges seem to reveal what you lack, roar back with the might of the resourcefulness you have within yourself, as that's truly all you need.

You possess a unique set of gifts. You have skills and experiences that are only of value once recognized. I once overlooked my own gifts, undervaluing and dismissing them. But if someone handed you a gift, would you sit there and let it gather dust? Of course not. Similarly, your talents shouldn't be sidelined. But it's up to you how you use your gifts, because you're not something that should be wasted.

The Self-Interview Assessment

Here's a straightforward exercise to help you recognize your unique gifts. It's called the Self-Interview Assessment. Start by writing down an exhaustive list of everything you bring to the table: your skills, abilities, experiences, qualifications, talents, hobbies – anything that reflects your own value. Don't hold back, and don't dismiss the small stuff.

Once you think you're done, push yourself to double the list. Your brain will try to brush past things or convince you they're not important – don't let it. Ask yourself questions like: *What have others said I'm good at? What challenges have I overcome? What makes me proud of myself?* When you've finished, read the list back as if you're evaluating someone who wants to be your business partner, closest friend or part of your inner circle. Would you be impressed? If the answer is no, go back and add more, because everyone has strengths – they just need to be acknowledged.

Finally, reflect on what stands out and what you might be undervaluing. This exercise isn't about inflating your ego; it's about finally seeing yourself clearly and understanding the value you have to offer.

Authenticity Attracts

Here's the thing about making yourself radically authentic and showing your real self. It doesn't drive people away; it brings them towards you. And the people it brings towards you aren't people who like the half-true watered-down version of you. They like the actual you. A couple of weeks after I had doubted myself when I overheard that comment in the bathroom, and before I'd decided to redouble my efforts to integrate all the different parts of myself – however negatively the world might view them – I got a message on Instagram from another coach, Liam James Collins. He was my age, covered in tattoos like me, and didn't fit the typical 'coach' mould at the time. We clicked instantly. Over coffee, we shared stories, and the similarities were crazy – not just because our goals and values were exactly the same for life and business, but because of our past traumas. Liam had also suffered abuse and had recently lost his dad to suicide. Yet, despite his grief, he radiated something so special. The best part was, we had two perfect pieces of business strategy that, combined together, would provide people with a way of creating true freedom in their lives.

Liam was actually once one of the youngest coaches in the world, as his mum was a coach too, and at sixteen years old he'd attended her training just to show her support and pack out the room a bit when she needed bums on seats. Liam had done various jobs, from actor to stockbroker to postman, but he had found his feet in the world of coaching and training and for the past few years before I met him he had been training people to become certified life coaches and neuro-linguistic programming practitioners. So, he trained people to become coaches, and I was helping coaches start and grow their businesses. We had the combination that would provide an end-to-end service to enable people to quit their job, learn a life-changing skill, help others, make money, and work anywhere in the world. Thus, The Coaching Masters was born. None of that would have happened without my willingness to be honest about my experiences – honesty that had caused him to reach out. It was every single thing about me, my story and my true personality that made him feel like our partnership would transform both of our lives and made him feel compelled to connect.

When we practise radical authenticity and integrate every part of us, however 'dark' or 'negative', we take so many things that could be seen as adversity and transform them into an asset.

Key Takeaways

- Vulnerability is a strength, not a weakness. Growth starts when you own your scars, fears and mistakes. Open up to allow others in.
- There is no such thing as 'normal'. It is exactly the things about us that aren't typical that can be our greatest strengths.
- Any negative trait can be a positive one when viewed from a different angle. Context and balance are absolutely key, but don't let others decide the box you get put in.
- Shadow work is a tool that can be used to integrate the 'negative' aspects of yourself. We are strongest when we learn to integrate – not suppress – these parts of ourselves.

- Stop conforming. There are some rules you should follow. But there are so many rules that shape our lives that aren't really rules at all. Life is too short to live by someone else's imaginary rules.
- Authenticity attracts the sort of people you want to have in your life.

So far, we've looked at a variety of techniques you can use to build up a true picture of who you are, how your mind operates, and how you can work out your deepest motivations and the mental blocks that get in the way of you achieving your goals. And in this chapter, we've looked at how a reframing of your negative traits can be transformative. But we've been focusing mainly on changing our attitudes and world view. In the next chapter we're going to focus on what can often be the hardest thing of all: action. And not just ordinary action, but raw, imperfect action.

CHAPTER 6

Raw Imperfect Action

This book almost didn't get written at all.

When I was first approached by my publisher, I was honoured. I could see immediately how it would bring together in one place so much of what I was learning. I knew there was a need for it. Every day I spoke to people hoping to develop in themselves and other people the skills that this book would contain. But every time I sat down, every time I looked at that blank page, I was overcome by a feeling of paralysis. I probably still had the voice of that Shakespearean hater in my head from the time I'd written an e-book. I also still had a mess of feelings left over from my negative experiences at school. Every time I'd write a sentence, I'd delete it. Write a different one. Delete that. With every day that went by, the pressure increased. Now each sentence had to be even stronger because I'd wasted so much time. Each word that got deleted meant the next one had to be exactly the right one. It had to be perfect.

I was dragged back to the same place I'd been in rehab, where every morning we'd had to submit our morning diary. I'd sit there, meticulously writing, but if I made even a single mistake, spelled a word wrong or smudged it, I'd rip up the page. I was petrified of people thinking I was stupid. Even if I couldn't see a mistake, I was certain there was one there. I stopped handing the diary in but was reminded that this was compulsory.

I was sat in my room, contemplating the idea that I might get thrown out of rehab because I was too scared to show I wasn't perfect, when I suddenly started laughing. I realized I was literally there because of a long list of mistakes, diagnoses and addictions. This notion I had that they expected me to be perfect suddenly seemed absurd. If there was a place in the world more used to working through people's mistakes than rehab, I couldn't think of it. So I got out my diary and I wrote down how I was feeling, with utter honesty. If I made a mistake, I crossed it out and left it there. It was the scruffiest, messiest, most crossed-out bit of paper you can imagine. And when it came time for them to respond, it got the most positive feedback I'd ever had. They didn't mention a single thing about the 'mistakes'. And I realized that my perfectionism was actually a manifestation of low self-worth.

Perfection is impossible. Holding yourself to that standard is the quickest way to never do anything. All those years later, I sat down at my laptop and I finally started to type. Words flowed, and a book was created, because of one shift of thinking, one act of bravery, one decision to be imperfect – and because of that, thousands and maybe millions get to receive the message that was almost destroyed through perfectionism.

Does any of the following feel familiar? You hold yourself to really high standards and feel constantly disappointed when you don't meet them. Every time someone in the group has to pick a restaurant or a holiday destination, you end up doing it and then feeling massive pressure that everyone else should have a good time. You keep hoping that other people in your life will step up and get it right, but they never quite do. Every birthday or Christmas present you buy isn't quite right. It wasn't quite enough effort, wasn't quite thoughtful enough. Do you constantly find yourself doing things because it's just easier that way? Do you find yourself crafting a version of yourself for social media? Retaking photographs, panicking if you didn't capture a moment that would have worked brilliantly as a post? Do you constantly compare yourself to high performers and find yourself feeling 'less than'? Do you focus on the small things that you don't do right, rather than the big things you do? Do you need everything to be perfect before you can complete a task? Do you need perfect silence, the right book with the right pen, before you can start to write? If there's even one tiny thing wrong, does it feel like things are ruined and there's no point even attempting the task?

If any of these things ring true, you are not alone. I would say that perfectionism is the number-one weakness people volunteer about themselves when you speak to them. Partly this is because it's one of those weaknesses that sounds like a strength. Along with 'working too hard' and 'caring too much'. But it's time to cut through the bullshit. Caring about what you do; having exacting standards; doing whatever it takes to deliver the very best of yourself in any given scenario. These are all fantastic traits. But let's be honest, perfectionism isn't about those things. Perfectionism is an excuse to stop yourself or others doing something by creating an excuse not to do it. It's your brain tricking you into inaction and framing it as a good thing. But it's not.

There's nothing sadder than the dreamers who never take any action. They are filled with ideas that make their eyes light up just talking about them. Yet they stay stuck in the same place, never putting those plans into action. They don't realize that the thrill of progress is addictive! When you see yourself move one step closer to your goal, you want more. Even just starting can create more momentum than you'd expect.

Here's a harsh truth: most people know what they need to do to change their lives, but they don't actually do it. It reminds me of a saying: 'They know what to do, but don't do what they know.' It's simple, but it's the difference between nothing and everything. It's the difference between having a map and making the journey. You can have all the directions in the world, but if you don't take the first step, you're just standing still, clutching a piece of paper.

Perfectionism is often a way of putting yourself at the centre of the universe if you have ever felt like you haven't been taken care of. Remember how voids form values? One of the classic ones is that anyone who grew up feeling unsafe, insecure or unloved will naturally find ways of protecting themselves by putting themselves at the centre of their own universe. Perfectionism can be part of this because it often has at the heart of it the feeling that everyone is looking at you and cares what you do. But here's a secret – no one cares. Now, that doesn't mean that no one cares *about* you. It just means there is no scary circle of people permanently waiting there to laugh at your mistakes. It's become trite-sounding through overuse, but 'dance like nobody's watching' is genuinely really good advice. Because you know what everyone is doing when it's time to dance? Worrying that everyone is watching *them* – not looking at you.

An important first step is to pause and ask yourself: *How often is the kind of criticism I'm imagining actually ever said out loud?* Honestly. We all worry about being judged, but when was the last time you heard someone truly tear into a person for trying their best and making a mistake? Sure, people can be rude, harsh or just act like dicks – and yes, it's fine to have standards. But most of the criticism we fear isn't real. It lives in our heads.

Now imagine your three-year-old daughter hands you the first picture she's ever drawn. Would you tell her the eyes are too far apart? That the hair's not right? That she forgot the nose? Of course not. You'd say, 'That's amazing, well done!' You'd smile, hug her, tell her she did a brilliant job – because you love her. You care.

Anyone who would pick apart a child's drawing like that? They're one of those Shakespearean haters – the kind of people who'd criticize the Mona Lisa just because they can. That says more about them than it ever will about you. And even if you did somehow redraw the Mona Lisa, they'd still have something to say.

The one person in a hundred who criticizes you doesn't matter. The other ninety-nine people will support you, lift you up and genuinely care – and those are the people who matter. But the most important person – the one who truly decides your worth above all else – is you.

What if the Hater is You?

That voice in your head, the one always judging, dismissing, picking apart – what if it's yours? Because often it's people carrying their own insecurities who end up projecting them onto others. Not out of malice, but out of pain. They're subconsciously trying to pull others down, just to make the climb feel a little less lonely. If you've done this – don't beat yourself up. We all have. Or even still do, at some level.

Admitting that someone else is doing better than you, or living a life you secretly want, can be hard to swallow. So instead of saying 'That's inspiring', we say 'That's cringe'. Instead of admitting 'I wish I had the courage to do that', we say 'They're full of themselves'. We project. We slap our own discomfort on someone else's face and pretend it's theirs. But here's the trap: when you see the world this way – through a lens of judgement – you assume others are doing the same to you. And because you think they're judging you, you judge yourself. And because you judge yourself, you judge others. And round and round it goes. It's a vicious cycle. And it never ends . . . until you decide to break it.

So how do you break it? It's simpler than you think. Become other people's cheerleader. Treat everyone like they're your three-year-old daughter, handing you their very first drawing. Tell them you're proud of them. That they did a good job. That they had the guts to create, to show up, to try. You'll be shocked what happens. First – you'll make someone's day. Second – they'll likely reflect that same energy back to you. But most importantly – you'll change the way you see the world. Because once you experience giving unconditional support and seeing that it doesn't weaken you – that it strengthens you – it rewires how you view others, and yourself. You stop assuming that flaws are failures. You stop thinking imperfection equals shame. You stop believing that every mistake must be punished. Instead, you start to see progress. Courage. Humanity. You start to believe that people are doing their best, including you. And just like that, the cycle ends.

How powerful is it to realize that you've always had the key, and the cage, in your own hands? You were in control the whole time.

Imperfect Action Wins Every Time

Remember back in Chapter 2 when we talked about building a growth mindset? Well, now it's time to put that theory into practice. Growth doesn't come from dreaming, planning, or waiting until something is polished. It comes from *doing* – messy, raw, uncomfortable doing. That's where the real learning happens. That's how ideas evolve. That's how businesses are born (and books get written).

The biggest lie we've been sold is that the best product wins. It doesn't. The product that launches first wins. The version that gets tested, tweaked and refined in the real world. That's what creates momentum. Speed beats perfection, every time. Because while you're still perfecting version one, someone else is already on version five – and improving with real feedback.

We get paralysed by the idea that our first version has to be flawless. But the longer you sit on something, the more likely it is to die in the dark. The truth is: perfection is just procrastination in disguise.

And if you need proof, let me take you behind the curtain of The Coaching Masters. When Liam and I first launched the business, we didn't have a ten-year plan. We didn't have a course. We didn't even have slides. What we had was an idea – and a Facebook Live. We told our audience we were running a live course starting on a specific date, and from that one livestream, we made £17,000. The catch? We hadn't created a single module. Why? Because we were testing. We wanted to see if the market *actually* wanted what we had to offer. And when people started signing up, the real feedback began. In the comments, they told us what was missing, what excited them, what confused them. So, we pivoted. We used those insights to build something better – not in theory, but live, in real time.

Every week for twelve weeks, we showed up with a handful of PowerPoint slides and delivered from the heart. We watched people's faces. We listened to their reactions. We saw where their eyes lit up and where they frowned in confusion. After each session, we'd hit pause on the recording and ask for honest feedback. *What did you love? What didn't land? What do you want more of? What's still missing?* That feedback shaped the next week. And the week after that. Until we had, by the end, a course that was built *with* them, not just *for* them. That raw, unscripted, imperfect course became our flagship coaching accreditation programme. And here's the crazy part: we still sell that same version today. Nearly a decade later, that original Zoom-recorded programme has generated millions and changed thousands of lives. We've talked about re-filming it. Making it slicker. More 'professional'. But every time we think about it, we stop. Because people love it the way it is. They love the authenticity. The imperfection. The realness.

What was meant to be a rough draft ended up becoming the masterpiece. And that's the power of imperfect action. If we had waited until it was perfect, we'd still be talking about our vision instead of building a global business.

So, the message here? Stop waiting. Stop planning. Stop tweaking that thing no one's even seen yet. Put it out there. Let it be a proof of concept. Let it be messy. Let your audience shape it. Let your experience sharpen it. Whether it's a podcast, a coaching offer, a social post, a workshop, a product or your next big idea – just *start*. The magic doesn't happen in your notes app. It happens when it's real.

Because every minute spent trying to perfect something is a minute stolen from progress. And the people who succeed aren't always the smartest or the most talented – they're just the ones who showed up and did it first. Start where you are. Use what you have. Refine as you go. And remember: imperfect action wins every time.

The Positivity and Perfection Illusion

As president, Barack Obama was a firm believer in the saying 'Don't let perfect be the enemy of good'. He made it one of the key pillars of how he approached the biggest job in the world. He knew that accepting only perfection was the quickest way to never get anything done. If we wait for perfect to come along, we'll be waiting for ever. More than that, focusing on the absence of perfection can become a source of negativity and resentment. Because you start to think that all those people out there who are doing things must be doing things perfectly. All those perfect people are doing perfect things while you're stuck in your imperfect life, doing nothing.

When you're constantly trying to be perfect or positive, you start to feel ashamed of your darker emotions or personality traits. Sadness, anger, fear – and jealousy, arrogance or irresponsibility – become dirty words, things to be hidden and suppressed. But, as we've discussed, those emotions are part of being human and ignoring them doesn't make them disappear; it just buries them deeper and causes more problems in the long run.

Let's take a moment to talk about the 'light' we all crave. The Mr or Mrs Perfect everybody pretends to be or wishes they could be like. We all know that image of perfection isn't real, and it's time to truly realize that. Life isn't all about running through fields of daisies. Sometimes it's like being stuck in a storm with an umbrella that just turned inside out and pretending you're not drenched. An obsession with positivity often leads to denial and avoidance. We're told to slap on a smile and keep going, even when we're breaking inside. Bottling up those negative emotions or darker traits is like shaking up a can of Coke and pretending it won't explode the moment you open it.

The self-help culture's overemphasis on positivity is like putting a plaster over a bullet wound. It might cover things up for a while but doesn't heal the underlying damage. Real healing comes from digging deep, facing the pain and working through it. It's about being brutally honest with yourself and recogniz-ing that it's okay to not be okay. It's okay to feel lost, broken or angry – and it's okay to acknowledge some of the less desirable things about your personality or the things you may have done in your past. And if you're going through the darkness right now, that's okay too!

Even if you don't complete something to perfection, you still did it. That will motivate you to do the next thing. Your capacity to achieve increases exponentially when your achievements don't have to be perfect. But here's the cheat code. Every time you try but don't get something exactly right, you'll still be getting better. Every imperfect thing brings you a step closer to perfection.

We all know that sick guilty feeling of not doing something we really know we should be doing. We can distract ourselves from it, but then suddenly we're reminded that we haven't done it – but this time it feels even worse because another hour or day or week has gone past. The feeling of raw imperfect action is the exact opposite of that feeling. It is an energizing, motivat-ing rush that propels you onwards. This doesn't mean that you should be slapdash and not care at all. But a couple of typos, a slightly wrong colour, a draft logo – these things won't destroy what you're trying to do. After ten years, I'm currently on my fourth website, third brand and second company name – but none of that stuff has stopped me from progressing my business. These are things you do, not things you are.

The Shatter Perfection Exercise

This exercise isn't just about letting go of perfectionism. It's about ripping it up, stomping on it, and proving to yourself that the world doesn't collapse when you lower the bar – in fact, it expands. Perfectionism is a cage. A slick, silent prison that looks like ambition but feels like paralysis. This exercise is your jailbreak.

Here's how it works. Pick something you've been procrastinating with – something you're avoiding because you're scared it won't be 'good enough'. A social media post. An email. A piece of content. Starting a project. Whatever it is, do it – but don't do it well. Deliberately complete it to a 'good enough' standard. No refining. No re-reading. No re-recording. Just execute and release it into the world. Then reflect. Did anyone notice the flaws? Did the sky fall down? Or did you finally feel free?

The purpose here isn't just to teach you that progress beats perfection. It's to rewire your tolerance for what's acceptable. And here's the truth most people miss: your standard doesn't shift gradually. It snaps. It shatters. Which is why you don't just need a soft nudge away from perfectionism, you need to blow it to pieces.

That's exactly what I did when I handed in a terrible diary entry to my rehab counsellors. Not average. Not slightly under-done. Badly written. Sloppy. Unstructured. Raw. On purpose. Why? Because I needed to destroy the false belief that my worth was tied to how perfectly I performed. I needed to shock my nervous system into realizing that doing something 'wrong' didn't mean I was wrong. I needed the evidence that I could mess up – and still be okay.

That one act didn't just challenge my perfectionism, it transformed my identity. And that's what this is really about – becoming drastically different, because in transformation, drastic is exactly what we're aiming for.

So, if you want to supercharge this exercise, don't just do something imperfectly. Do it badly. I mean messy. Rushed. Full of typos. A video with bad lighting and no second takes. A caption that rambles. An email with spelling mistakes. Put it out there, knowing it's rough.

Because when you do, and the world doesn't end, you'll feel a kind of freedom most people never access. And the best part? When you return to your usual standard, you'll realize how far your ceiling has stretched. You'll operate with less fear, more flow, and unshakable proof that you are the one in control – not your perfectionism. This is how you break the illusion. This is how you take back power.

Confidence as a Choice

Stepping into the realm of imperfection is often linked to what is perceived as a lack of confidence. The first thing you need to know is that you *are* confident. Sometimes, we need to hear it from someone else before we can believe it ourselves. The number-one thing that stops people from being confident is saying, 'I am not a confident person.' This is just one of the stories your brain has learned to tell itself. And when you say that, you're assuming the identity of someone who isn't confident and can't be. This mindset prevents growth because you're limiting yourself.

Put simply, if you feel you're incapable of confidence, you will never experience it. I used to say to myself, 'I'll never change.' But I realized that beliefs, attitudes and behaviours can change, and it all starts with believing they can. If you keep telling yourself you aren't confident, you're absorbing that message into your subconscious. Instead, tell yourself a new story: 'I am a confident person.'

Act As If

One powerful strategy I've learned to build confidence is to 'act as if'. This technique is not about pretending to be something you're not, but about stepping into a version of yourself that embodies the confidence you aspire to have. For example, I've had previous clients with low confidence, so I ask them to stretch their perspective and act as if they think they're better than everyone else. Their challenge is to act arrogant for a week. Now, at first glance, that might sound like a strange or even counterproductive exercise, but there's a method to the madness. What actually happens is that these clients never come off as arrogant. Instead, they display what most people would recognize as normal, healthy confidence. Their perception of arrogance is skewed by their own insecurities, and this exercise helps them recalibrate their internal sense of true confidence.

This approach works because it gives people permission to push the boundaries of their usual behaviour. When you're used to acting small or second-guessing yourself, the idea of being confident can feel foreign, even arrogant. But by 'acting as if' you already have that confidence, you begin to shift your mindset and, in turn, your behaviour.

Another similar tactic is to create an alter ego that is a confident persona you step into when needed. This isn't about faking anything; it's about tapping into the qualities you already have but maybe haven't fully embraced yet. Think of it as borrowing confidence from another version of yourself. When you adopt this alter ego in social situations, or when facing challenges, you can bypass your usual self-doubt and act with a level of confidence that might surprise you. Having an alter ego helps you break free from the habitual patterns of self-doubt. When you operate under this persona, your usual insecurities and fears don't have the same grip on you.

For example, if you've always been reserved in social situations, creating a naturally outgoing and self-assured alter ego can help you step out of your comfort zone. As you continue to adopt this persona, you'll find that the confidence you once had to 'borrow' starts to feel more like your own. The lines between the persona and your true self blur, and you naturally start to embody the confidence you once thought was out of reach. It's like trying on a new outfit – it feels strange at first, but the more you wear it, the more it feels like your own.

You can also build confidence by challenging yourself to take confident actions. Start with something small, like messaging a stranger on Instagram, and gradually work your way up to something bigger. For instance, one of my clients, who once was terrified of singing, started by singing to a couple of her friends and ended up taking a speaker and singing in the streets of London. Confidence is like a muscle; it will grow the more you use it.

Empowerment through Ownership

I remember a time when I was a kid, and I was tidying my room, and then my dad walked in and said, 'Tidy up your fucking room!' And just like that, something switched in me, and I decided I wasn't going to do it any more. The reason? The moment someone else takes ownership of your actions, it feels like the choice isn't yours any more, and that's when resistance kicks in. It wasn't about the task itself, but about the fact that it no longer felt like my decision.

Taking ownership of our actions is everything. We're

empowered and motivated when we feel like the choice is ours. But the moment someone else tries to dictate our behaviour – even if it's something we actually want to do – our inner rebel emerges. It's human nature. No one likes being told what to do. Society floods us with expectations. You 'should' have a stable job. You 'should' be married by a certain age. You 'should' fit into this box or that one. It never ends. But those 'shoulds' are someone else's script, not yours. Following your own path means letting go of what's expected and choosing what's right for *you* – even when it doesn't make sense to anyone else.

This doesn't just happen with others. We do it to ourselves too. How often have you caught yourself saying 'I should be doing this' or 'I should be doing that'? It's like you're lecturing yourself, and trust me, your mind reacts the same way it would if someone else were telling you what to do. Instead of driving action, it creates resistance, and you end up stuck, battling your own stubbornness.

The same goes for 'need'. Now that one can feel really heavy! How many times have you caught yourself using that one? It's guaranteed to overwhelm you, and you haven't even finished the sentence so your brain thinks of the worst-case scenario. It will jump to 'I need to do this, or I will die'. The key is to bring yourself down to reality and help fill in the gaps in your brain in a less stressful way. It's also important to remember that there is nothing you really *need* to do. You can do whatever you want. If you want to sit in front of the TV your whole life and do nothing, that's your choice, but if you've chosen to do something else, that doesn't mean you need to; it means you want to!

Words shape our reality, and the way we talk to ourselves can either ignite our motivation or douse it completely. Instead of using words like 'should' and 'need', which feel like an obligation, swap them for something that gives you back control. You can say 'I want to' or 'I'm going to'. This small shift in language will make a massive difference in how you approach things.

Here's my favourite reframe: 'I get to'. When you say 'I get to', you're also adding a layer of gratitude. Then, it's not about what you have to do; it's about what you're privileged to do. You're shifting from a place of resistance to a place of appreciation. So, next time you catch yourself using 'should', pause and reframe it. Make it your choice.

Taking Action

The next step is to put that awareness into action. We often get stuck in a loop of overthinking and analysis paralysis, where the fear of making mistakes or not being perfect prevents us from taking the necessary steps towards our goals.

I once heard a story about a man who attended a high-priced mastermind seminar only to disappear into his hotel room after a few hours. Despite the costly ticket, he didn't resurface until the end of the event. It might seem crazy to us, but the man had his strategy. Once he'd found a nugget of wisdom that he could apply to his business, he knew it was more beneficial to act on it than to continue trying to consume more information. What golden nugget of wisdom could you apply right now?

Too many people are stuck in procrastination mode due to over-analysis. Analysis leads to paralysis. When we overthink, we scare ourselves out of action. But remember, progress demands movement. If you want to move from where you are now to where you want to be, you've got to take action. Taking action is the heart and soul of development.

Of course, planning and preparation are important. You don't want to charge ahead blindly. But they should only be a part of your journey. Ultimately, it's your actions that will lead you to your destination, not your plans.

Understanding what triggers your procrastination is a key step in overcoming it. Reflect on the times you procrastinate – whether it's when a task feels too overwhelming, you have no idea where to start, or when you overthink. By identifying these triggers, you can work on ways to address them directly. One way is to realize it's a trigger holding you back, and decide to dominate it: count down from three and just do it! Whatever it is. Yes, it's as simple as that. Think of the task – 3, 2, 1, GO!

The Art of Goal-Setting

Let's talk more about goals. Not the vague, wishy-washy kind you scribble on a to-do list and forget about the next day, but real, actionable goals that will change your life. Analysis leads to paralysis when we overthink, but goal-setting is an important part of achieving those life-changing goals. Most people don't reach their goals not because they lack ambition, but because they use the wrong approach. Thinking about what you want and jotting it down is fine in theory, but without clarity, emotion and a proper plan, that list will just gather dust while you stay stuck. The reality is, some days, you won't feel high on life and ready to tackle your challenges. Success doesn't happen overnight. Sometimes it occurs in small measures, but the bigger results take time.

People often refer to me as an overnight success. However, it's taken ten years to get to where I am today. Yes, there were huge wins along the way, but they also compounded over time. This fits perfectly with a quote by Bill Gates: 'Most people overestimate what they can do in one year and underestimate what they can do in ten years.' I often see people getting deflated due to a lack of short-term results, and letting their old beliefs consume them and pull them back to where they started – when really, as simple as it sounds, all they need to do is have the mindset to keep putting one foot in front of the other, and they will be amazed at where they arrive if they just keep going.

Imagine yourself trying to hit a target. Now imagine doing it with a blindfold on. You don't know what the target looks like or where it is. It's the same with goals. Without clarity, you're just hoping for the best – and hope doesn't get results. To hit your target, you need to see it clearly, understand its shape and aim with precision.

Think of this next exercise as goal-setting on steroids. It's designed to strip away the fluff and get down to the specifics of what you want, why you want it, and exactly how you'll make it happen. By the end of this process, your goals will be so clear and emotionally charged that you won't just want to achieve them – you'll be driven to.

Setting Your Goals

Positive framing: First, focus on what you want, not what you don't want. Your brain is terrible at processing negatives. What happens if I tell you not to think of a blue balloon? You think of a blue balloon. That's why it's so important to phrase your goals in the positive – because if you don't, you might start to accidently work towards the opposite. Instead of 'I don't want to feel stuck any more', try 'I want to feel energized and motivated daily'. Shifting your focus to what you want puts your mind on the right track from the start.

Sensory evidence: Now, make your goal real. A goal without a sensory connection is like a house without a foundation. Imagine what achieving your goal will look, sound and feel like. Close your eyes and picture it. What will you see when you've achieved it? What will you hear? How will it feel? The clearer and more vivid this image is, the stronger your belief will be that it's possible.

Context: This is where you get into the details. Where is this goal happening? What's going on around you? Who's involved? For example, if your goal is to run a marathon, where will it take place? What does race day look like? Who's there to support you? These details make the goal feel real.

Timeframe: Without a clear timeframe, your goals become open-ended, and that's a recipe for procrastination. Pin down the specifics. When will you start? When will you finish? How much time will you dedicate to it each day, week or month? Having a timeline creates accountability and gives you a sense of urgency.

Resources: Every goal requires resources, whether internal, like confidence or patience, or external, like tools, skills, or support from others. Identify what you need to make this goal happen and how you'll get it. This isn't just about making a plan; it's about ensuring the plan is realistic and achievable, and that you have everything you need to achieve your goal without excuses.

Personal connection: This is a big one. Ask yourself: *Is this goal really mine? Or is it something I think I should do because of external pressure or expectations?* Goals that don't resonate on a personal level are hard to stick to. Be honest with yourself. Why does this goal matter to you? How important is it on a scale of 1 to 10? If it's not a 10, what would need to change to make it a 10? The stronger your personal connection, the easier it'll be to stay committed when things get tough.

Purpose: Finally, remember your values and how they come together to create your big 'why'. Without a strong purpose, even the clearest goal can lose its power when challenges arise. Ask yourself: *Why do I want this? What will achieving it mean to me? How does it align with my values?*

Plan: Finally, make a brief plan of action. Although you may not know exactly how to achieve your goal yet, write out a rough list of five steps that could get you there. Don't worry, these can change over time. But the most important thing is the first step. Make this first step a 'must' – and commit to doing it, with no negotiations, at a specific date and time. Then off you go! Make it happen.

Here's the hard truth: dreams are easy. They're nice to think about but really mean nothing without a plan. Goals are clear, emotionally charged, and backed by strategy. That's the difference. A dream is just a thought. A goal is a commitment. By applying this model, you're not just setting a goal but creating a roadmap to actually completing it.

Start with the Short Term

Ideally now you'll have zeroed in on your long-term goals based on your core values. But sometimes we need a little lighter fuel to start the fire. And that's where proving others wrong can be an excellent source of raw imperfect motivation. It probably isn't the best long-term source of motivation, but it is a source, nonetheless. Of course, I can advocate for the motivational sources that are healthy, but if you're looking for results, negative motivation can be powerful, too. It taps into our need for significance and recognition, and I have experienced this myself – at first, everything I did was to prove my dad wrong. I even had a poster on my wall for a couple of years that read, 'Sometimes I feel like giving up, and then I realise I have a lot of motherfuckers to prove wrong.' I'd like to say I've matured a lot since this time, but hey, it worked, and I'd put it back up on my wall again if I needed it.

Has there ever been anybody who told you that you couldn't do something, or wouldn't make it, or laughed at your ideas? Maybe it was a teacher at school, an ex, or Slimy Karen across the road that irritates you because you know she thinks she's better than you? Have all their faces in your head when you feel like giving up. Keep pushing forward, and, ah, man, when you do succeed, you won't need to say a word to them; they'll see, they'll know – and I can't lie, it feels great.

Beware of Run-Ups

An aspect of searching for perfection that I often come across is the desire to take a really long run-up. A great example of that in my own life was when I came back from travelling and decided I wanted to go to university. It had been such a dream of mine and was such a big part of my sense of identity that it felt utterly essential. But three months into a four-year course I started to feel like there was such a gap between what I was learning through my business and what I was learning at university. I was still giving everything to the process, and there was this nagging voice that I had to stay at university, had to get the qualification, I had to commit to it, put the time in. But one day, I had the realization that this was just another form of perfectionism. Don't get me wrong, education can often be the right thing for people. Learning is absolutely essential. But we can sometimes use external markers of readiness as an excuse to avoid doing something.

We all know people whose lives are organized by the things they're going to do once this or that thing is out of the way. But what happens when that thing is done? There's always another thing to take its place. I started to see that I was like a long-jumper constantly on the run-up. At some point, you have to jump. If you wait for the perfect time, you will wait for ever. So, I left university and went all in on my business. I took the extra time and energy I had been putting into my studies and invested them into my career – I started gobbling up more content, enrolled in training courses, and hired coaches and mentors. It utterly transformed my business.

Sometimes, keeping your head down, paying your dues and building knowledge, skills and experience are the right things to do. After all, you can't jump very far without some sort of run-up. But always ask yourself, is there any chance you're allowing yourself to keep running because you're scared of jumping?

Kill the Imposter

Let's discuss 'imposter syndrome'. This is like carrying a backpack full of doubt, and no matter how much you achieve, that load never seems to get any lighter. It's the nagging voice in your head telling you that you're a fraud, that you don't really belong here, and sooner or later, everyone will find out. It's not just self-doubt; it's a deep-seated belief that your success is built on luck, not skill, and that any moment now it will all come crashing down. Imposter syndrome doesn't care who you are or how much you've accomplished. You could be the CEO of a Fortune 500 company or just starting out in your career – it doesn't discriminate. It thrives on the fear that you're not enough and that you've somehow tricked everyone into thinking you're competent, and that eventually your so-called luck will run out.

The annoying thing about imposter syndrome is that it often hits hardest when you're on the right path. It's like your mind testing you, seeing if you're really up for the challenge. It whispers that you're not good enough, smart enough or deserving enough, but the good news is that imposter syndrome is nothing more than a mirage.

Of course, it feels real, but it's just smoke and mirrors. You're not an imposter – you're simply human. High achievers are often the most susceptible to it. Why? Because they set the bar so high for themselves that anything less than perfection feels like failure. The reality is that the only way to stop yourself from feeling like an imposter is to stop thinking like one and lower the bar. Even if you have big goals, take a moment to acknowledge where you are now, the sacrifices it took to get there, and the fact that you deserve this even if you decide to strive for more. Call out imposter syndrome for what it really is: a fear response, not a reflection of reality. Remind yourself that nobody has it all figured out.

Imposter syndrome is usually a sign you're stepping into new territory, pushing boundaries and growing, and that's exactly where you're meant to be. Say the words 'I am', followed by your chosen identity. The only person who can question your choice is you, so be sure you're rooting for yourself. Once you've decided, start acting the part. Before you know it, you'll start to become that person. It's a bit like 'fake it till you make it', but I prefer 'be it till you see it'. Yes, it might feel uncomfortable to suddenly decide you're a 'successful entrepreneur' or 'someone deserving of love'. But it will bring you closer to achieving that just by stating it.

Key Takeaways

- Perfectionism isn't a badge of honour. It will convince you it's not worth doing something if it's not flawless. Progress comes from showing up, trying and learning, not trying to be perfect. Imperfect action beats perfect inaction every time.
- Confidence isn't a personality trait; it's a decision. Stop saying 'I'm not confident' and start acting like you are.
- Dreams stay dreams until you take action. Overthinking kills momentum, while small steps create massive change. Don't wait for the perfect time or all the answers – they rarely come. Start now, focus on doing rather than planning, and let the progress build.
- Goals are not just ideas; they're commitments, and they need clarity, emotion and a solid plan to bring them to life.
- Imposter syndrome is just a sign you're growing. The voice telling you you're a fraud? It's lying. High achievers feel it because they set the bar high. No one feels 100 per cent ready all the time.

By learning all the ways our brain tricks us out of taking action, we're building a toolkit, not just of awareness but of power. Every time you spot the patterns, every time you move forward imperfectly instead of staying stuck, you're now moving forward. But it doesn't stop there. If you can do that with your thoughts and fears, you can do the same with habits, routines and patterns that you live by every day. Because let's be honest, most of us are running on autopilot, and those default settings are rarely geared towards our highest potential. So, in the next chapter, we're going to look at how to strip out the harmful habits that are holding you back, install the ones that will move you forward, and start designing your life with intention so you can reclaim your time, your focus, and ultimately your life.

CHAPTER 7

Obliterate Your Habits

'And for you, sir?'

The waiter at the restaurant, co-working space and coach training centre I have created looks at me expectantly. I imagine one of our perfect curated cocktails, the ice cubes just starting to melt and crack. The condensation on the glass. That first sip as it burns on my tongue then down my throat. The feeling that will spread through my whole body, of peace and relaxation.

'Apple juice for me, please.' The waiter smiles and walks off. Neither he nor anybody else around me knows how much effort that took. Of course I want a 'proper' drink. To reward myself for all of my hard work. We have just launched Café Coach. It is the pinnacle of years of hard work and every part of my being is screaming that I deserve just one drink to celebrate. But I know that, for me, it is never one drink. For me, it is the first step on a road that leads to disaster.

That road led me to waking up in a hospital bed in my mid-twenties, as a doctor told me that if I kept on drinking and taking drugs like I was, I would be dead by the time I was thirty. It led to lost nights, days, weeks, months and even years. I have done my time at the coalface of addiction. I have learned to understand that I am an addict and always will be.

But I have also seen the power of addiction from the other side of the fence. In my late teens and early twenties, I became

173

involved in drug dealing. It began small. A bit of coke here and there, more for friends than anything. Then came meow meow – legally a plant fertilizer but a euphoria-inducing drug in the underground scene. At first, it was legit; I even had promotional flyers! But then it was made illegal, and that's when the real challenge began. The game was high-stakes, with high rewards. Deliveries from Glasgow, cutting, repackaging, the whole operation. The enterprise grew, and at its peak I had several people working on my line, and sometimes making £3,000 or £4,000 a week. In prison, pretty much everyone I spoke to had some sort of connection to addiction. This has given me a powerful insight into its terrifying power. When someone is locked in that relationship, everything else fades away. All they can focus on is the next hit. It is the ultimate example of focusing on an external thing to fix us, despite all the available evidence.

Addiction is the Solution

Addiction has to do with drugs and alcohol – and at the same time, it has very, very little to do with drugs and alcohol.

There are addictions that don't involve any substances at all. People become addicted to behaviours. To relationships. To validation. To chaos. To control. It doesn't have to be something you snort, sip or smoke. Addiction is about what you turn to when you can't sit with yourself. But here's the deeper truth that most people miss entirely: the drug isn't the problem. The drug is the solution.

Yeah, it's a solution that ruins lives, destroys relationships, tears families apart and often ends in death. But it's still a solution. A temporary one. A destructive one. But one that *works* in the short term to numb what's really going on underneath.

That's why it's so hard to let go of. Because, for a moment, it offers relief.

So, if the addiction isn't the real problem, then what is? It's whatever hole you're trying to fill with that addiction. It's the pain underneath. It's the discomfort of being in your own skin. It's the shame you can't name. It's that restless energy in your chest that won't let you relax, even when you can't pinpoint where it's coming from. It's the feeling of being on the outside looking in, no matter how many people are around you. It's the quiet belief that you're fundamentally broken. That you, on your own, are not enough.

That's what people are trying to escape from. The drug is just the delivery system. And even if you're reading that and thinking 'that's not my story', let's consider things from a different angle. Because we all have a compulsive relationship with something. Maybe it's not alcohol. Maybe it's food. Maybe it's spending. Maybe it's your phone. Maybe it's sex, or work, or drama. Maybe you can't stop chasing people who treat you badly, or putting bets on every time there's a match, or bingeing shows you don't even enjoy just to drown out your own thoughts. Maybe you can't stop refreshing your inbox, hoping that next email will finally make you feel good enough. Maybe you go shopping for clothes you'll never wear, or doomscroll your way through the night until your eyes sting. Maybe you're chasing the next goal or career move in the hope it will finally make you feel like you've arrived. That you're complete. Whole. But it doesn't, so you keep searching, looking for your next fix, when deep down it's you that feels broken, even if you don't know it.

The point is you don't have to be shooting up heroin every day to be an addict. It's just the stigmatized or more negative addictions that get the most attention due to the destruction they cause. But if you're scrolling through your phone all night while making your partner feel unappreciated or ignored, or they perceive it as a lack of love that causes a breakdown in your relationship, you will understand that other addictions can be equally as destructive. We all escape into something. We all reach for some kind of fix. And at some point that fix becomes the trap. *That's addiction.*

Now, the chapters in this book so far should already have started to guide you towards your truth. You've begun to connect with your authentic self. You've explored your shadow. You've started to understand and accept parts of you that were hidden for years. And when you truly know yourself – when you can sit with your pain without needing to run – you no longer need an external solution to fix an internal problem.

But let's be honest, this doesn't shift overnight. Self-connection takes time. Sometimes we need to start on the surface before we can go deeper. Sometimes we need to create space to think clearly, to heal, to breathe, before we can get to the real stuff.

In this chapter we'll explore how to begin changing the habits that keep you stuck. We'll look at ways to remove the symptoms of addiction so that you can finally begin tackling the real cause.

And one vital note before we move on: if your addiction is to a substance or substances, I want you to put this book down and seek professional help. I know from bitter experience how high the stakes can be. This is one area where I really have to repeat that this book is in no way a substitute for expert care. Get the help. Then come back. The rest of this book will be waiting.

Reset Your Rewards

Our brains are wired to push us towards doing things that help us survive. That's why eating, having sex, and spending time with people we like tend to feel good – and why pain, rejection and conflict usually don't. Deep inside our heads is something called the 'reward system' – a complex bit of biological kit designed to release feel-good chemicals when we do something the brain sees as beneficial.

The reward system can be hijacked. Substances, habits, even certain emotions can mess with it, triggering compulsive behaviour and, over time, literally changing the way the brain works. The science behind it is deep, but at its core it's simple: the brain gets a hit of chemicals when we do something rewarding. There's serotonin, which helps with long-term happiness. Endorphins, which cause that rush when you've had a great laugh or smashed a workout. Oxytocin, the 'love hormone', released when you connect deeply with someone. And then there's dopamine.

It's all tied to pleasure, reward, motivation, achievement, novelty, and even just the *anticipation* of something good. The brain loves it. But it's a bit of a diva. It likes its rewards immediate, guaranteed, and preferably physical. That matters, because it explains a lot about why we chase the things we do.

Here's the problem. When you repeat a dopamine-releasing behaviour often enough, your brain adapts. It starts expecting it. Craving it. And the more it gets, the more it wants. The baseline shifts. What used to satisfy you no longer hits the same way, so you go harder, or more often. And now you've got a loop. You're not just doing something to feel good any more – you're doing it to feel *normal*.

That's why certain cravings pop up in specific situations. Sitting on the couch with Netflix might spark the urge for wine. Getting on a train home might trigger the itch for a pint. Reaching for your phone when you hit an escalator – yep, that's dopamine too. That tiny flash of anticipation that someone might have messaged you – that's the hit. And when nothing's there, it's like the balloon deflates. You feel flat, anxious, even a bit lost.

The cycle reinforces itself every time you give in. You strengthen the connection between trigger and reward, and over time those brain pathways literally deepen. The more you respond, the more automatic it becomes. And that starts to bleed into everything. It gets harder to make good choices, because the brain's priority isn't what's best – it's what's *fast*. That's why you reach for your phone instead of replying to that important email. It's the path of least resistance. It's the shortcut to feeling okay.

But here's what I want you to really take in: this isn't about willpower. You're not broken. You're not weak. You're running on biochemistry – and so is everyone else. The good news? You can rewire your brain. Once you understand how your habits work, you can not only start letting go of the ones that don't serve you but also build the ones that do. This isn't just about cutting back; it's about choosing the kinds of rewards you want to build your life around. You can train your brain to crave progress, connection, growth, fulfilment. It takes time – and yeah, it takes patience – but it works. You're not alone in this. And more importantly, you're not stuck.

Finding Your Habits

The first thing you need to do is take an honest inventory of your behaviours. Start by asking yourself if there is anything you currently do more than you'd like, and is it taking away time and space from things you want to do more of? It can be useful to break down your day. What do you actually spend time on? Write everything down – every time you check your phone, every time you open your laptop. Every packet of crisps, every biscuit. It's often in those moments of downtime that our brains will have formed triggers that we aren't even aware of.

Once you have a list, start to think about how you would feel if someone said you couldn't do one of these activities. Notice the ones that make you feel panicky or angry. Because anticipation and triggers are such key aspects of the reward system, it can be useful to try to 'trick' your triggers.

To come back to the beginning of the chapter and that drink at my own bar . . . I understood that this was a connection that had formed in my brain between celebrating and having a drink. But I had learned how to have plenty of good times without alcohol. It was just a leftover connection I needed to tidy up. So every time I started to picture that cocktail, I didn't try to ignore it, instead I concentrated on imagining a tall, frosty glass of apple juice. I imagined a boiling hot day and being desperately thirsty. I put the two images on top of each other in my mind, like layers in Photoshop, and slowly turned up the opacity on the apple juice until it completely replaced the cocktail. All that was left in my mind was savouring every drop of that refreshing apple juice.

But I didn't stop there, because I knew myself too well. I added in the pride that everyone in my life who I cared about would feel when I chose the apple juice over the alcohol. I added in how good it would feel to wake up sober, not with a dry mouth and a thick head. It wasn't easy, but I kept doing it, every time I felt a trigger, and I was able to replace one behaviour with another.

It's not a magic trick, I still have cravings. And it means I can only go to bars that serve apple juice. But it's worth it.

Rebalance the Decision

Should I go to the gym or stay in bed? Should I stay for one more drink, or be sensible? Shall I make a salad or order in pizza? This is a simple exercise you can apply the next time you are faced with a moment of decision where there is an element of reward or comfort involved. Remember your brain wants you to do things that reward you. But also remember it likes rewards that are immediate, tangible and certain. Think about how often in life our long-term goals – the ones we really want to accomplish – are the exact opposite of this. Saving up for that life-changing trip versus buying that amazing pair of jeans. Getting into shape versus the doughnut that's *right there*.

A lot of the time, your brain is actually not a great judge of what will actually bring true long-lasting rewards. Most of the time it tends to massively focus on the short term and be much less focused on medium- and long-term rewards. That's why it feels so much easier to look at your phone than do that work task you're putting off. Although the payoff for doing it would probably bring you much greater satisfaction overall, it feels distant, abstract and you might not even complete it. The tiny hit available through the game on your mobile is right there, right now, and definite. Your brain is weighing up decisions without the load of the weight. So your job is to add that weight back in.

Next time the alarm goes off and you lie there and think, *Bed or gym?* – don't just leave it at that. If your brain has to choose between your lovely comfy warm bed and getting up, in the moment, let's be honest, it's probably going to choose the bed. Instead, focus on all of the pleasures that going to the gym brings. That satisfying burn in your limbs, the sense of starting the day off right. Be honest – have you ever regretted going to the gym instead of not getting up? Remind yourself of this.

Connect this one gym session to your long-term goal of getting in better shape. Remind yourself of why you want to get in shape – whether it's because of that beach holiday you have coming up, or so that you live longer for your kids. Or do the opposite, and factor in the negatives of staying in bed. During a seminar I attended, 'Unleash the Power Within' with Tony Robbins, we did an exercise where we visualized both positive and negative outcomes. This was called 'the pain and pleasure principle'.

Sometimes, it's important to envision a future where you have not achieved your goals. By imagining the pain of a future where you remain stagnant, you can push yourself into action. Ask yourself: *Where will I be in ten years if I don't change? How will my relationships, health and financial situation look? What opportunities will I have missed out on?* It's like accounting for a whole invisible set of costs.

Now revisit the decision to get up or not. I bet it feels totally different now. And you can do the same thing when faced with any decision of this sort. Any time you're going to give yourself a treat or avoid something you know you really should do. Start to factor in all the things your brain isn't very good at. Add the forgotten weight into the decision and feel the scales tip the other way.

Long-Term Ammo

A really useful exercise is to arm your brain with ammunition to combat this imbalance. So, for every long-term goal you have, you need to add detail. Don't just think 'get in shape', give it detail and make it as fully imagined as possible. Think about all the things that will come with getting in shape. Imagine yourself proudly walking down the beach next time you're on holiday. Imagine all the things you will be able to do – like playing football with your kids. Imagine the sound of their laughter. Use all of your senses. But also make sure you look all of the negatives of not getting in shape in the eye. Make them concrete, make them specific, make them emotional. Write it all down, somewhere you'll see it. And then the next time you're weighing up whether or not to go for a morning run, go through all of the reasons. The decision is completely transformed. Because you've added back in all the weight to the other side of the scales.

Of course, we all have a whole set of things we do that we don't really notice making decisions about. These are called habits. Not all habits are bad. You don't agonize over whether to brush your teeth every time – whether you fancy it or not, you just do it. That's because that habit is a well-worn pathway in your brain. To understand how we can use that to our benefit, we have to take a very quick look at our brains.

The Habit Brain

Your brain has come together over millions of years of evolution. Rather than being one thing, it's a whole complex web of systems, the vast majority of which are not conscious – that is, you do not have to actively think about them. You don't have to think about what your heart rate, or blood pressure, or breathing rate should be (though now you've thought about it, weirdly you will have to think about breathing until you forget about it again). You don't need to decide when or how much your pupils dilate, how much you sweat, or do anything to digest your food – your brain is handling all of that for you underneath the surface. When you grab the handle of a hot pan, or something flies towards your eyes, your brain takes evasive action before you have a chance to think about it. As we saw earlier, the fight-or-flight reflex occurs at a level way below consciousness. Like an iceberg, the vast majority of what your brain is doing happens beneath the surface. Some people estimate as much as 95 per cent of your brain's total activity is unconscious.

Then there are things that we do so often that they become pretty much automatic. If you drive a car, you may have had that experience of arriving home and suddenly not remembering how you got there. Reading and playing musical instruments, or learning the complex button combinations for your favourite computer game. Things that begin in our conscious brain can make their way into our subconscious. We can use this to drive positive habits.

Our habits are not set in stone. Because of the magic of neuroplasticity, we can create environments in which we are more likely to do more of the things we want to do and less of the things we don't. James Clear sets out a very clear framework in his international bestselling book *Atomic Habits*.

To Build a Good Habit and *To Break a Bad Habit*

1. Make it obvious | Make it invisible
2. Make it attractive | Make it unattractive
3. Make it easy | Make it difficult
4. Make it satisfying | Make it unsatisfying

So, make the fruit bowl easier to see than the biscuit tin. Then, when you're choosing between an apple or a chocolate biscuit, make sure to think about how you'll feel. Don't just leave it down to what you fancy – your brain will almost always choose the quick, easy hit of processed sugar in treat food – add information in that makes one more attractive than the other. Think of the consequences of picking one over the other. You could even write it down on a sheet of paper and keep it near the biscuit tin.

Dead Time or Drive Time

What is your morning like at the moment? If it's the shock of the alarm followed by a rush to get out the door, you are not alone. But what if your morning commute could be the moment everything changes. Let's get real. Most people spend their commute either dreading the day ahead, scrolling aimlessly on their phone, or just staring out the window half-asleep. It's dead time. But what if you could flip that time into the most powerful, productive part of your day?

What if you wake up and the first thing you do is reach for . . . your notebook. A lot of people charge their phone next to their bed and it's the last thing they look at and the first thing they pick up. I'm not here to judge anyone, but what if you tried charging your phone in a different room and made the last thing you touched and the first thing your notebook in which you plan your day?

Swap the doomscrolling or silent suffering for an audiobook, podcast or educational series that actually grows you. It sounds simple, and it is, but don't confuse simple with insignificant. Some of the biggest turning points in my life have come from the tiniest moments. A single sentence once hit me like a punch to the gut: 'Enjoy the journey.' Another one? 'Stop being a consumer and start being the creator.' Those words didn't just sound nice, they sparked action. Suddenly I was building new habits, challenging old beliefs and moving differently in the world. And it all started while sitting on a train.

Information at the right time can change everything. But you've got to be open to receiving it. Most people are numbing out during their commute. You don't need to do that. You could use that time to rewire your thinking, upgrade your mindset, and literally absorb years of wisdom on your way to work.

Let's break it down. The average UK commute is about 56 minutes per day round trip. Multiply that by the working calendar. That's roughly 220 hours per year. That's the equivalent of a six-week training course you never even had to book time off for. Imagine what could happen if you used that time to listen to thought leaders, coaches, business minds or even neuroscience experts. After a year, you wouldn't just be motivated, you'd be dangerously capable. In the top 1 per cent of knowledge in your niche. And nobody would even know what you were doing differently. They'd just notice you changing.

So, here's the challenge: reclaim your commute. Stop wasting it. Whether you're on a train, in the car or walking to work, plug into something that feeds your mind. That 'dead time' might just be the moment that wakes you up.

Keep it going throughout the whole day. We all have so many daily moments when we could be stacking habits onto what we already do. Whether that's getting into the habit of checking your task lists every time you check your email, to make sure you're not escaping into email as a way of avoiding your larger goals. Or maybe it's as simple as swapping in reading an article for online shopping or the social media doomscroll of shame.

However you do it, the key is to focus on small, achievable tweaks to your routine that get you closer, step by step, to the activities you want to do more of. The trick to building habits is repetition, so a small, achievable change you're going to actually keep at is much better than a big change you only do a couple of times or never at all. The mistake we often make is to try to do too much, fail and let this demotivate us. Remember, don't let perfection be the enemy of raw imperfect action. You don't have to make this enormous change to offset all the times you haven't before. Start with setting one tweak as a goal, and then congratulate yourself when you succeed. Add another positive habit from a position of triumph, not guilt and failure. When we celebrate our small wins, we activate our habit loop and this win is factored into our behaviour in the future.

It can often be easier to amend an existing habit than delete one entirely. A common mistake we make with new year's resolutions is that we either want to start an entirely new thing or stop a pre-existing behaviour. Instead, we can tweak behaviours that already exist. You're far more likely to succeed by swapping in healthy options bit by bit in different parts of your life than just writing 'Stop eating junk food' on a bit of paper.

Make the change specific. Order the salad rather than the fries next time you get a takeaway. Charge your phone one night a week in a different room to the one you sleep in. If you can deal with that, try two. Go for a run twice a week. If that works, up it to three times. Start small, succeed, and build it up. These changes might start out small, but the total effect can be enormous. You get more done, you feel better, your brain feels sharp and clear. Instead of a vicious cycle, you will find yourself in a virtuous circle.

Hack Your Program

Another useful technique is something called Implementation Intentions. This is where you explicitly link a situational trigger to a response you want to do more of. So, rather than saying to yourself 'I want to go for more runs in the morning', you say 'If it's 8 a.m., I go for a run'. And instead of saying 'I want to eat more fruit and vegetables', you say 'If I'm watching a film on the sofa, I'm eating carrot sticks'. This works because it actually takes your brain less effort to process your motivation; it's just a kind of mental computer program that produces a response. If you are specific about a date and time for something you want to do and frame it as a certainty, you are far more likely to actually do it.

It's also been shown that sharing this plan with others makes you more likely to do it. It's why sparring partners, spin classes and run clubs are so useful. They are regular events that you sign up for. The small commitment and public aspect mean it's easier to keep to these arrangements than to a vague promise to 'go to the gym next week'. Remember, this isn't about willpower. You aren't a bad person for finding it hard to stick to habits when you don't understand them. You've been given a brain that is brilliant at some things but isn't really designed for so many of the situations you find yourself in.

The Two-Minute Rule

A good way to start can be through practising the two-minute rule. This means, instead of trying to change a big habit all at once, you break it down into things that take no more than two minutes. So, make it a habit that you read one page of your book before bed. Or you wash one dish when you pass the sink. You open your letters as soon as you receive them. You make your bed as soon as you get out of it. Admiral William H. McRaven has written a whole book called *Make Your Bed* about how important small, disciplined actions are for setting the tone for your whole day.

Track, Track, Track

A key aspect to doing more of what you want to do and less of what you don't is tracking. Tracking our actions helps make them concrete rather than abstract. This is key, remember, because we want to activate the brain's reward system and it responds much more strongly to rewards that are immediate, tangible and certain. We can utilize this in making sure our environment is optimized. So, if you want to read rather than look at your phone, leave a book on your pillow. Leave your yoga mat where you can see it from the sofa. Put your jogging water bottle out on the kitchen table the night before. These sorts of concrete triggers use up less of your brain's processing power, and so your brain actually finds it easier to do them.

Then, when you do these things, track, track, track. Whether it's through a diary, an app or a website, track your wins and celebrate them, loudly. Your brain absolutely loves progression, success and achievement. Something as simple as a tick in a box or a smiley face or a pixelated fireworks display is enough. It will reinforce the habit loop and make it more likely you'll do it next time. Remember we are all, deep down, apes pushing sticks into rotten logs and hoping we come back with a grub to eat. Give your brain the reward and it will want to do the thing again. And if you don't quite make a goal, record how close you came to getting there. There's a big difference between 'failed' and '67 per cent completed'. There is no right or wrong way to do this – the only goal is progress.

Tracking your results also allows you to see patterns. Is there always a particular day, or series of days, when you find it harder to tick those boxes? Why might that be? What is going on? I have had clients who swear by tracking every element of their lives, including how much energy they have before, during and after certain tasks. They then organize their lives to make use of this, performing sequences of tasks when they have the most energy. I'm not saying everyone should do that, but tracking brings the invisible into the light and then you can do whatever you want with it. It also holds you accountable. Because we all have days when we fancy a lie-in, or have had some news that we need to focus on. The key is to get back into the routine you want to have, as soon as possible. That old advice to 'get back on the horse' is rooted in science. You need to make sure that any 'failure' is a temporary setback, not a new lot of patterns and habits, as there's a danger you'll just stack negative habits on top of the positive ones. Track the failure – draw a red cross rather than a tick, then get on with filling the rest of that page full of green ticks.

Turn Hard into Normal

Preparing yourself for some hard work is vitally important. Anybody who tells you that change is easy is lying. However, it doesn't always need to feel so hard. 'Hard work' is a phrase that depends on our individual experiences, isn't it? What we deem as 'hard work' right now could well be the norm in the future.

Let me take you on a quick trip down memory lane to the bustling streets of Cambodia. I remember this guy there who converted his moped into a taxi called a tuk-tuk, his lifeline and a ticket to survival. Each day, he'd shuttle tourists around the city for a solid twelve-hour stretch, navigating the chaos with an unshakable spirit. But the end of his driving shift didn't mean he could crash and go to bed like the rest of us. Instead, he'd go to a hotel and slip into his second role, a night receptionist. Curiosity got the better of me, and I asked him about his sleep. His response: 'I don't worry about sleep; I just want more experiences.' He told me that he stole naps in the gaps when tourists were out exploring. What struck me wasn't just his nonchalant acceptance of his crazy routine but his focus on the experiences he was collecting rather than the lack of sleep. Now, I'm not advocating that anyone reading this should cut down on sleep, but it was a real eye-opener . . .

This work ethic isn't unique to him; having lived in Asia for five years, I've discovered this is normal for many people there. Early mornings, late nights, and barely a murmur of complaint. This got me thinking: *What makes them so resilient? Are they born with an extra dose of stamina?* But the truth is simpler yet powerful. It is about adaptation. For some, their circumstances require them to work those long hours to scrape together enough to survive. Thus, the notion of 'hard work' is just different for them. Their 'normal' is our 'hard', but it is just life to them.

We, too, have the capacity to redefine our threshold of hard work, and to adapt and evolve. If what feels hard today could become our new normal tomorrow, then growth isn't just an option, it's an inevitable part of our journey. And who knows, with this mindset, we might even start viewing these challenges as enriching experiences, just like my Cambodian friend did.

Take a moment to reflect on what 'hard work' means to you right now. How does your current definition influence the way you approach challenges? Think back to a time when something that felt difficult eventually became part of your normal routine – what helped you adapt and grow? Now, consider how you're viewing your current challenges. Could you shift your mindset to see them as opportunities to grow stronger or more capable rather than just obstacles? What habits or skills could you start building now to make today's struggles easier to handle in the future? Finally, ask yourself if your focus on how hard things feel is stopping you from noticing the progress you're already making, or the opportunities that might come from pushing through. By reflecting on these questions, you can start redefining what 'hard work' means and recognize your ability to adapt and evolve.

Cut the Crap, Get More Done

When I say you need to work hard, this doesn't mean immediately throwing yourself into eighteen different things at once. Multitasking is fine for cartoon octopuses but it's bad for the human brain. This is because of something in the brain called 'task-switching'. Basically, when you move back and forth between tasks, you waste time and energy on starting up, whereas if you stay at one task for longer, you get more done using less resources. The worst thing is that the more we task-switch, the more energy we use up trying to do it. This leads to slower and less creative decisions and poor memory. There have even been studies that multitasking may change the actual physical structure of the brain. It also, and we all recognize this, just feels more stressful, with all of the associated negative aspects of stress.

Supercharge Your Productivity

It's not just about breaking habits for the sake of it, it's about maximizing your efficiency, and there are all sorts of simple, practical ways you can optimize your brainpower and productivity. The first is planning and tracking what you do. I'm a big believer in to-do lists. I have them for the day, the week, the month and the year. For me, it means I don't have to use up any processing power on keeping that stuff in my head. It's like adding extra memory to a computer. If you don't do this, your brain is wasting so much background power just worrying about the shapeless mass of things you have to do. We've all had that experience of a task we've been dreading for weeks suddenly being done in five minutes. It wasn't a big deal at all. But it felt enormous. Planning and tracking start the process of removing as many of these distracting tasks as possible, and leave your brain to focus on more of the stuff that matters.

Stop Worshipping the Ping

Let's be real, most of us aren't brain surgeons. Most emails don't need a reply in sixty seconds. Yet here we are, twitching like addicts every time a notification pops up. That's not productivity, that's digital people-pleasing. Even worse, that's chasing the feeling of completing a task, but we're not actually doing the work when we're replying to emails within ten seconds. Take a step back. There might be times in your working day when you need to check in and see if anything urgent has come up. So set times in the day where you check messages, then get ruthless. Outside those times, the world can wait. If someone's bleeding out, they'll call, and if they don't, it probably wasn't that urgent.

Deep Work, Not Busy Work

We all like to feel busy. It makes us feel important, it makes us feel like we matter. But if we're totally honest, we can all fall into the trap of spending our time on tasks that don't matter but give the feeling of being busy; we're spinning our wheel on shallow tasks that feel important but don't actually move the needle. This is comfort disguised as productivity. Instead of doing ten things at 10 per cent, try doing one thing at 100 per cent. Give your brain permission to dive deep. No bouncing between tabs. No 'just quickly' checking WhatsApp. Block out ninety minutes to concentrate on one thing.

Make a list of everything you need to do, then start to rank them. What's going to make the biggest impact on your life or business? And what's the thing you're most avoiding because it's uncomfortable or hard? That's your number one. Do that first. That's your dragon. Go slay it. Trust me. You might feel like you want to warm up a bit. Practise on a troll or a couple of goblins. Nope. Right this minute, worrying about facing the dragon is taking up so much valuable space in your brain – and once it's out of the way, everything else will be easy in comparison. Kill the dragon and take that momentum with you for the whole day. Productivity isn't about doing more. It's about doing what matters.

Work Like You Fight

Work at high intensity, in short rounds, with full focus, then rest – just like a professional fighter. Then, get back in the ring. All in, gloves on, head down; nothing else exists. Then pause. Get up. Shake it off. Breathe. Walk it out. That's your corner break. Then go again. It's like stepping into the next round.

Treat your focus like a fighter treats their energy – with respect. Don't waste punches shadowboxing with distractions. Save your power for when it counts. Go in hard, then step out to breathe. You don't win fights by dancing around all day. And you don't win in life by half working with one eye on your phone and the other on your inbox. Victory comes in the moments you're fully switched on, throwing everything you've got at the task in front of you. Get in the ring. Go for the knockout. Rest. Then do it again.

This isn't about hacks. It's about reclaiming your time, your energy and your headspace. Because the goal isn't just to get more done – it's to get the *right things* done with your whole self in the game.

When you learn how your brain works at the most fundamental level, you can game the system and use it to create more of what you want in your life – and less of what you don't. You reverse the polarity on that black hole of addiction that sucks everything else into it and you create a big bang of positive behaviours, throwing good habits out into your personal universe and using productive and efficient techniques to make more meaningful progress in your life.

Key Takeaways

- Your brain is set up to reward certain activities and behaviours. The more you understand it, the more you can rewire it to your advantage.
- Your brain likes quick, easy, certain rewards. You need to learn to rebalance your brain so that you make decisions that are actually the best ones for you.
- It is much more effective to adapt an existing habit than stop it or start an entirely new one. Learn how to augment habits by stacking them.
- 'Hard work' is relative and adaptable. What feels difficult now can become your new normal. With the right mindset and consistency.
- Ditch multitasking. Prioritize high-impact work, focus in short intense bursts, and protect your mental energy.

A key aspect of rewiring your patterns and staying consistent is involving other people – and not just for accountability reasons, but because helping others fuels real, lasting change. What we call the 'helper's high' is one of the most powerful reward systems we have.

When you use your own journey to lift someone else, you don't just heal them, you heal yourself. As you move into the next chapter, you'll see how the real path to becoming unlimited isn't just transforming your own life, it's about helping others do the same.

CHAPTER 8

Giving to Grow

'How can *you* be a life coach?'

When I was starting out, I would often face that question. Back when I was still trying to convince enough people to pay a £30 subscription to cover the cost of renting a community hall, and tea and biscuits. I remember marching into the local newspaper in Portsmouth and announcing that I was launching a budget-friendly life coaching business that was going to change the world. Instead of kicking me out, they said they could do a photoshoot for an article. This was my big chance. There was one problem – I didn't have a suit. So I sprinted to the nearest Next and grabbed the first suit I found – a beige one. Then I had to be careful not to get anything on it as we did the photoshoot, as I had to go back and return it because I needed that money to live on. There I was, admittedly looking like a Jehovah's Witness rather than a coaching guru, but there on the front page. But then I have always looked very different to the typical life coach.

At that point, the life coaching realm was full of shiny Americans with perfect teeth and a California tan, who looked like they'd been grown in a lab somewhere. Here was this bloke with tattoos everywhere, who'd made every mistake going. Suddenly he was going to start telling people what they should do? *How does that work?!* It's a fair question. In fact it's the number-one question that the little voice in your head asks when you start to think about becoming a life coach. To be honest, if you don't ask yourself that question, it's probably a worry. If you're sitting there thinking your life is the perfect exemplar that everyone else should follow, you're almost certainly not growing. You're sat smack in the middle of the comfort zone. I have never believed it's the people like that who make the best coaches. I want people with pasts. Who have made mistakes and have the scars to prove it. Because it's in facing adversity that we learn what matters.

I believe that facing adversity and making the decision to help other people change their lives is a kind of superpower that unlocks a person's full potential. I have seen, time and time again, that the things we do to become the best coaches make us better versions of ourselves. I've seen it so many times. Someone signs up for coach training thinking they'll learn a few skills to make money or help others, and they end up having their entire world turned upside down. I'm not exaggerating. I remember the very first cohort of one of our courses – our coaching accreditation. At the end, we recorded their testimonials, and I still watch those videos sometimes – there are tears, breakthroughs, lives changed. These weren't just people ready to start a business. They were people who had found a completely new version of themselves.

But what really *is* coaching? Most people would mumble something about 'helping people achieve their goals', and yeah, that's part of it, but it's just scratching the surface. Coaching is about transformation that is real, lasting and often unexpected. It's a partnership, not a dictatorship. It's not about being the expert or even giving advice; it's about guiding someone to unlock the answers they already have inside them.

I remember when someone posted on one of my Facebook ads once: 'What can I learn from you? You look about 12.' I was actually twenty-eight at the time, but I did look younger before I grew a bit of facial hair. Anyway, this was my response:

'If you got to know me, you'd realize I've been through more in my "12 years" than some do in a lifetime. But coaching isn't about how old you are or what I can teach you. It's about how I can support you in getting results. Grey hair and years of experience don't automatically guarantee success. What truly matters is knowing the tools, techniques, and frameworks that create real transformation.'

When you coach, you're not there to *fix* someone's problems. You're there to create a space where they can explore their own thoughts, gain clarity and take meaningful action. You're not their teacher, their mentor or their therapist. You're the facilitator of their growth – the person who asks the questions that make them go, 'Damn, I never thought of it that way.' This is where people often get it wrong. Coaching isn't about teaching someone how to do something or sharing your wisdom. Teaching is transferring knowledge. Mentoring is guiding someone based on your own experience. Therapy is about resolving trauma and understanding behaviour. Coaching? It's none of those things. Coaching is future-focused. It's about helping people figure out what they want, why they want it, and how they'll get there. You're not there to give them the answers. You're there to help them uncover the answers on their own by asking the right questions. When someone discovers their own path, they own it. It's theirs, and that's what makes it stick.

The beautiful thing about coaching is that it changes you as much as it changes the people you work with. As you learn to coach, you become more self-aware, more empathetic, and more in tune with what matters. You start showing up differently in your own life. Coaching isn't just a skill; it's a way of being. It's a mindset, a way of seeing the world, and a way of interacting with people that lifts everyone up, including yourself. Though I had been successful in my previous coaching ventures, it was when we focused on training coaches that things really exploded. It also became clear that developing the skills to help other people live their best lives is something that transforms both people in the coaching relationship.

To understand why, we need to uncover the truth about altruism.

The Altruism Myth

Altruism is silly, if you ask me. It means helping others by giving your time, money, energy or support without expecting anything in return. Why would you deny yourself time, money, energy or support? They're life's most valuable things, and essential for a fulfilling and sustainably rewarding, freedom-filled life. Think about the last 'selfless' thing you did – whether it was a favour for a friend, volunteering your time or donating to charity. How did it make you feel? Good, right? I think we waste a lot of time on altruism – this idea of a pure, completely non-selfish act. When it comes down to it, helping other people feels good. Other people noticing us help other people feels good. Rather than agonize over whether something is truly selfless, I think we should just concentrate on what makes the greatest number of people help each other. The fact that helping other people makes us feel good is a *good* thing. Because, as we saw in the previous chapter, our brain is constantly searching for rewards. And approval from our peers is one of the biggest naturally occurring sources of reward chemicals in our brain there is. Oxytocin? Tick. Dopamine? Tick. Endorphins? Tick. Serotonin? Tick. Kind acts are the full bingo card of our brain's feel-good chemicals.

So even at a purely selfish brain-chemistry level, why would you turn your back on that? The problem is that, when our own lives are tough, we tend to focus on ourselves at exactly the wrong time. Research has shown that something as small as holding the door open for someone, or giving them a compliment, releases reward chemicals in the brain. This isn't just some touchy-feely thing. It's science.

There are studies that have shown that acts of kindness lower the stress hormone cortisol, which also leads to better medium- and long-term decision-making. There are even studies that suggest it lowers blood pressure and reduces the risk of heart disease. The chemicals released when we carry out acts of kindness can lower our ability to feel pain. Other research has demonstrated that our immune function increases, as well as our longevity.

Helping others also strengthens our social relationships, which are an essential element in feeling good. More than that, the act of helping someone else raises our own self-esteem. When we feel useful, we feel better about ourselves – and when we feel better about ourselves, we make better decisions.

What I love about life coaching specifically is that it brings together these rewards – there is the satisfaction of doing a job well, and on top of that you are being paid for it. For some people that aspect of it can feel odd, but it's one of the first things we talk about at The Coaching Masters. Many of us feel an impulse to help other people for free. After all, isn't that the right thing to do? Isn't charging for it wrong? In fact, it is my strong belief that when you're compensated for your time, energy and expertise, you see the value in what you share and gain the resources to grow your platform even further. You also deserve it – you didn't learn all these lessons in life and potentially go to hell and back just to give it away for free. And even if you did want to give it away for free, people often don't value what is free: it stops them from taking it seriously, taking action, and they can lose interest. A saying we have at The Coaching Masters is: 'When people pay, they pay attention, and it works best when they invest.'

However, you don't need to become a life coach to benefit from feeling good by helping others. A key first step in my personal development journey was volunteering with a charity when I left rehab. When you realize that you can help other people, when you feel needed and like your presence is making a difference, it builds your self-esteem and confidence. Since then, I've had the privilege of speaking in prisons, schools and orphanages, and even travelled to Uganda to help families and homeless street children. Each time, I walk away with a deeper sense of purpose and connection – and, most importantly, gratitude and perspective on what matters and what doesn't. It's not just about what I can give, it's about what I learn and how I grow in the process.

A Fresh Perspective

As we've already discussed in the book, it can be easy to see what changes other people might be able to make in their lives that aren't possible at first with ourselves. And this is because of the stories our brain tells us to keep us safe. Without those stories in place, we can see the situation in a much more structural way. Always be alive to the advice you give when someone is facing a similar situation to you. What feels like the obvious solution? Why does it feel like something they can do but something you can't? Is it that you're thinking of their situation with the coach's voice but your own with the critic's?

You don't need to do anything with this realization. Just notice it. It can be incredibly useful to shift focus onto someone else and concentrate on their situation with your conscious brain. Because it often sparks your subconscious brain into action. It's like a healthy version of displacement. Think of it like putting something on the back burner for a bit. It's simmering away, ready for when you have time to deal with it. And if we practise this in our own lives and help others do it in their lives, the ripple effects are enormous.

Pay It Forward

This idea was popularized by the 1999 novel *Pay It Forward* by Catherine Ryan Hyde, but I first came across it in the film adaptation, starring Kevin Spacey and Helen Hunt. It's about a kid who comes up with the idea that every individual should do a good deed for someone – and then ask them, instead of repaying the favour, to do three good deeds for strangers, and then in turn ask those three strangers to do the same. The idea is that the ripples from these deeds spread out, touching the lives of far more people than anyone can individually. I remember watching that film when I was a kid and feeling like it was soppy and unrealistic. But these days I can see the appeal. Because there is power in taking action. Rather than seeing being kind as a passive act that is somehow about ignoring what you want, I have reframed kindness as one of the key ways to get my reward circuits firing.

Think of it like taking your brain to the kindness gym. Paying it forward and doing a good deed for someone, starting the day with a 'helper's high', is like a heavy workout session. Notice that the act of giving makes you feel like someone who has enough to be generous. And when we feel generous, we feel good about ourselves. Again, don't think about this as something you 'should' do – a rule imposed by others. Take ownership over your actions, and admit that doing a good deed for someone else is at least partly rooted in the benefit you will feel. Make your peace with that, and see it as one more way you can trick your triggers and benefit from your brain's reward circuits. Let it drive you to do more good in the world. Because, at the end of the day, the world needs more acts of kindness, no matter where it comes from.

At our lowest, it can feel as if the universe is a cold, selfish place, where everyone is out to screw everyone else over. By giving to grow, we help to create a world that is the opposite. One in which we encounter random acts of kindness. But more than that, if we can find a way for our purpose to align with helping others, it will supercharge our sense of purpose. Because then it isn't just about finding what lights *you* up, it's also about using that fire to light the way for others.

When you help someone else, you're not just being a good person; you're becoming a role model. This doesn't just benefit them; it builds you up too. Every time you help someone overcome something, you'll be reminded of why you're on this journey in the first place. You're also held accountable for what goes on in your own life when you know that others are looking up to you as a source of inspiration. They become a form of motivation. Once you are a role model to others, you aren't just making decisions for yourself. And you're far more likely to act in a way that makes those that look up to you proud.

I have witnessed first-hand how the incredible community at The Coaching Masters inspire each other every day. Each person is a mentor and a student at the same time. Learning and teaching, helping each other, and at the same time helping themselves.

Self-fulness

Another word for altruism is 'selflessness'. Which I think is another problem I have with it. Why would you do something that makes yourself disappear? Surely you want to encourage positive behaviours that are the opposite of that? That are the expression of your self, not its removal. Too often advice on altruism is big, vague and abstract. We know by now that any goals need to be concrete, specific and achievable. So the first step of self-fulness is to let go of the grand gesture and start with the small everyday things that we can all do a bit more of – that make the world a better place and improve our own lives and self-esteem simultaneously.

You can practise self-fulness through daily acts of kindness. These are small, everyday things that don't cost you anything – not your time, money or energy – but they leave someone else better off and fill you up in the process. There is zero downside; it's a total win-win.

1. **Give up your seat:** Someone's standing, and you're sat? Offer the spot. Easy. Instant lift for both of you.
2. **Let someone go ahead of you:** In the queue, in traffic, wherever. You lose thirty seconds. They feel seen.
3. **Send a kind message:** Text someone just to tell them they're doing great or that you're thinking of them. Unexpected kindness is powerful.
4. **Smile at strangers:** Not in a creepy way, just a warm 'I see you' kind of way. Human connection is underrated.
5. **Leave a positive comment or review:** Instead of scrolling past, say something good. Whether it's about someone's post on social media, a small business, or a podcast – share love, not silence.

6. **Hold the door open:** Classic, timeless, and somehow still rare. Makes you feel decent. Makes them feel considered.

7. **Pick up one piece of litter:** It doesn't have to be your mess to make a difference. Good for the planet, good for your mindset.

8. **Compliment someone properly:** Skip the surface stuff. Be specific. Tell them something real – about their energy, their work, their effort.

9. **Give genuine praise behind someone's back:** Say something amazing about someone when they're not around. It finds its way back to them – and that hits different.

10. **Leave a kind note:** On a mirror, a desk, a stranger's windshield, or even on your partner's pillow. A little 'You've got this' can hit deep.

And here's the thing most people don't realize: kindness has a ripple effect. That small act you did for someone? Chances are, they'll pass it on. Not because they have to, but because it feels good. And if you continue to carry out these small acts, it builds something inside you. A sense of being proud of who you are.

You don't need to open a school in Africa to make a difference. Sometimes the small stuff can make the biggest impact at the right time and shake someone's world a little. You never know what people are going through. You don't know if that person was feeling invisible or on the edge. But in that moment, they felt seen. And that can flip a switch. How powerful is that? You don't need to be a hero. You just need to be kind. Because when you are, you might just change someone's day, their outlook – or who knows, their life. And that . . . that's something to be proud of.

But let me hit you with the eleventh act of kindness which is at the heart of human connection, is invaluable when someone needs it, and is something anybody, and I mean anybody, at any time, can do.

Listen.

But this isn't just your usual listening, it's *active* listening.

Radical Listening

One of the simplest yet most life-changing things you can do each day is to simply listen. Not just hear someone, but *truly* and *actively* listen. I like to call it radical listening. Make them feel heard. You'd be surprised how many people go through life without ever experiencing that. The shift that happens when someone gets to speak their truth for the first time can change everything – for them, and for you. Watching someone feel understood, maybe for the first time in their life, is powerful. And knowing you played a part in that? That's transformation on both sides.

I bet you're thinking: *This is ridiculous, I know how to listen. I do it all the time.* But you'll be astonished by how a few simple techniques will transform your interactions with people. Because, without realizing it, even if you aren't aware of it consciously, many of us treat the time when someone else is talking as something to get through before it's time for us to talk. And even if we are genuinely listening, sometimes we're giving out signals that we're not.

A great small way to start is to try to use active or radical listening. There are a variety of techniques and acronyms, but I have always found the framework developed by sound and communication expert Julian Treasure especially useful: RASA, or Receive, Appreciate, Summarize and Ask.

When we **receive** it's important to signal that by making eye contact (I know for many non-neurotypical people this might not be easy) and by facing our bodies towards them. We should also make sure we aren't fiddling with our phones, or trying to do something else at the same time. A key act of listening is showing the person talking that you are listening. It's obvious to you, but to them any sense that you are only half listening will devalue the process.

When we **appreciate**, we are showing them that we value what they are saying. Too often, we might try to talk about a time that something similar happened in our lives. But it's key that to begin with you give nonverbal and verbal signs that you want them to keep talking. You can also say things like 'interesting' or 'go on'.

Summarize means that we essentially say the key parts of what has been said back to the speaker. This kind of detailed engagement with what is being said to you will show that you have truly listened and you hear them compassionately.

Finally, we can **ask**. This is where we deepen the conversation with open-ended questions. You'll notice there's no 'S' for 'solution'. One of the biggest barriers to active listening is the urge to fix things which might feel obvious to you. But this is exactly where active listening becomes most powerful.

Because listening isn't just about exchanging information. It's not about using the time the other person is speaking to plan what you'll say next. It's an act of generosity. An energetic offering that shows them that what they're experiencing matters. Often, people aren't looking for answers; they're simply longing to be understood. And by acknowledging their experience, rather than trying to fix it, you give them far more than any quick solution ever could – especially when it's not your issue to fix in the first place.

This is why counsellors and therapists ask questions and remain quiet. All therapeutic conversations place the speaker at the centre. A good active listener is creating a safe space where people can offload and process their thoughts out loud. And often, just doing that opens new pathways in the brain. When those pathways are accompanied by your thoughtful questions, seeds are planted. And while those seeds might not bloom immediately, it's in that space – gently held, unforced, without pressure – that realizations, breakthroughs and changes happen.

It's Okay to Want to be Acknowledged

Another thing about traditional altruism is that it shouldn't be about doing things that make you look good. We've already seen how important it is to make use of how our brain works. And caring what others think of us is one of the most deeply rooted urges there is. As we've already touched upon, having good relationships with those in our social circles could be a matter of life and death. So why would we turn our backs on this urge and repress it? Why don't we tap into it instead?

I do things all the time because I hope they will make me look good. I don't apologize for that. I celebrate that we live in a world where doing good things gets you social credit. It's something to be proud of and you deserve the recognition for doing it. If you're ever surrounded by people for whom doing good things doesn't get you credit, that's a red flag and a sign that you might need to change up your circle.

To be absolutely clear, all of this doesn't mean just talking the talk. You have to show up and actually do the good things. But if one of the things that motivates you to do so is the good feeling that other people will think well of you, don't beat yourself up over it. The main thing is that the good thing gets done.

The Cycle of Support

I'm living proof of what the cycle of support can create. Over a decade ago, I was a broken addict hanging on by a thread. But because a few people had the courage to reach out their hands and help me when I didn't even know how to help myself, I learned the value of giving a hand to someone else.

That's what started it all – just buying strangers a coffee and asking if there was anything I could do to help them. I didn't charge them. I just showed up and gave what I had. And what came back to me – whether you call it karma, the universe, God, or just the law of energy – was bigger than anything I could ever have imagined. Not in my wildest dreams – and I'm not just talking about a free coffee in return . . .

I'm talking about The Coaching Masters, a business now valued at $25 million and generating an eight-figure income, with more than 13,000 paying clients in eighty-seven countries. We've built VR- and AI-powered coaching tools, our own social networking app, and have physical locations in Bali, Mexico, and soon Dubai and London. We're an ICF-accredited training provider – holding retreats across the globe, and delivering international speaking gigs, including a TED Talk, features in *Forbes*, countless podcast interviews, magazine and newspaper articles, and even live TV appearances. Our podcast has racked up over a million downloads. I've starred in movies. I completed a PhD in Transformational Education Management, I've been featured in a top-ten charted Netflix documentary about my life. Our community has turned into a global family. Dozens of people have even tattooed our logo on their bodies as a permanent reminder of the transformation we helped create. And somehow, I've found a way to travel the world while doing it all.

None of this would've happened without helping people. Some might see that as bragging. I see it as pride. And I hope by the end of this book, you'll be ready to scream your wins from the rooftop too, because you'll know you've earned them.

Not bad for a so-called psycho, eh? And if someone like me can do it, with my past, my pain and every reason not to succeed, then so can you. Not just change your own life, but change thousands more in the process.

The more you give, the more you get. People will help you and you'll help people, and that's how the world should go round. That's how I see it, and I hope this book makes you see it the same way too. And if you want proof of how powerful that cycle really is, let me tell you about Lisa.

Lisa was the counsellor who once sat with me in a rehab centre and broke me down in the best possible way. She was one of the people who cracked me open enough to cry about my dad and finally start healing. Years later, I was scrolling Facebook, and her name popped up. I dropped her a message: 'Do you remember me?' I expected a vague reply, maybe a 'sort of', but she hit back with: 'Of course I remember you, Lewis.' I asked what I was like back then. She said, 'You were like a lost little boy who just needed someone to care about him before he could care about himself.' It stopped me dead in my tracks.

But it didn't end there. Lisa went on to *join* The Coaching Masters. We trained *her* to become a coach. The woman who helped me change my life now gets to help others using the tools we taught her. The last time she'd seen me, I was stomping around in a tracksuit, angry at the world, refusing to do the dishes. Now I got to help her step into her own purpose. That's not just full circle – that's a whole new orbit.

And if that weren't enough, I also went back to HMP The Mount – the prison where I once served time – and gave a talk with the very RAPT team that had helped me transform behind bars. I stood onstage, looked those inmates in the eye, and showed them what freedom after prison *actually* looks like. The same team that once guided me had invited me back to guide others.

That's the cycle of support. Give. Receive. Repeat. And the more you put into it, the more it will give back. Not always right away. Not always how you expect. But always, without a doubt.

Keep helping. Suddenly, other people stop being a source of adversity and become one of the biggest possible assets. You never know what lives you'll change – including your own.

Key Takeaways

- Helping others helps you. Coaching, kindness and contributions to the world trigger a chemical reward system that improves your mindset, confidence and health – while creating real change in someone else's life.
- Purpose is found through service. You don't need to be perfect to make a difference. Use your scars, not your status. When you help others rise, you rise with them.
- Coaching is transformation, not information. It's not about giving advice – it's about asking the right questions, holding space, and helping people find their own answers.
- Small acts create massive ripple effects. Whether it's donating, volunteering or simply listening, one small deed can spark an exponential impact.

- 'Reputation' isn't a dirty word. Wanting to be seen doing good doesn't make it less good. Own your impact. Be proud of it. And surround yourself with people who respect you for showing up.

You've experienced how giving to others fuels your own growth and creates ripple effects that touch every part of your life. But what happens when your progress is disrupted and challenges arise? In the next chapter, we'll explore what we do when the shit hits the fan, and how navigating setbacks is a vital part of your journey to becoming unlimited.

CHAPTER 9

Success Despite Setbacks

'You're a very lucky man; you could have died.'

Waking up in a hospital bed in Bali, the sound of a heart monitor beeping, I don't feel very lucky. I feel like I've been hit by a truck.

'You had a cardiac arrest. If it wasn't for your wife giving you CPR, there's a good chance you would have died.'

I glance to the side of me, where Dayana, my wife is sat, her eyes ringed red with tiredness and tears. We met when I found myself addressing a crowd on a stage in Barcelona. Amidst the sea of faces, Dayana stood out. As I unravelled deeply personal stories from my past, traumas included, I couldn't peel my eyes away from hers. Post-event, we connected the millennial way – Instagram DMs. Our days were straight out of some romantic film. Bathed in the Barcelona sun, we indulged in tapas and marvelled at the Sagrada Família. Then days melded into nights, and just three days in I dared to ask her if she'd stay with me and travel the world. We hopscotched from London to Paris, Dubai to Spain, and eventually settled in Bali. At this time The Coaching Masters was going from strength to strength. We were doing world-class work and it was being recognized. These had been the happiest years of my life. Four years after first seeing each other in Barcelona, we exchanged vows in the city where we'd met.

But one night my old thinking crept back in and I convinced myself I was okay to have a drink. Who am I kidding – I had been drinking for a while. Ever since we had received the news that our unborn baby girl, who we'd named Mia, wouldn't survive birth. For obvious reasons, the idea of becoming a father, of having that role in someone else's life, was for me not an uncomplicated one. But I had become so excited about becoming a dad. And then, after our scan, we got the news that is every expectant parent's worst fear. We held a funeral and that's when I started drinking again.

Those weeks and months are a blur. The grief was like a series of blows raining down on me, constantly. I spiralled out of control. The night before I ended up in hospital, I'd had an epileptic fit and blacked out before my heart stopped. That wasn't even the end of it. When they prescribed me drugs to help with my relapse, I abused those too. All those years of staying clean and sober, and here I was again. I felt myself teetering on the edge of an all-too-familiar urge. The urge to annihilate myself with drink and drugs, to escape these unbearable feelings.

And that is where everything I've talked about in this book so far really came into play. It's easy when things are easy. The true test is what happens when things get hard. And this was about as hard as things had ever been. Every fibre of my being was screaming at the universe. How unfair this was. How unlucky. Those familiar patterns still there, underneath all the work I'd done. But this time I had a toolkit. And one day, I found myself looking in the mirror and I made the decision. It was time to go again.

I wasn't sure whether to tell this story. It is still incredibly raw. One of the darkest moments in my life. I'm aware that I was not the only one feeling grief, and that allowing myself to collapse under that weight might be seen by some as a selfish act. But I want to be completely honest with you, because I believe that we are not defined by our mistakes.

The first thing I had to do was stop taking the easy way out. Because everything I've said right from the beginning of the book is still true. But when something disastrous happens, our brains will use it to try to go back to those old stories. *See, you tried so hard, and through no fault of your own it all went wrong. So what's the point of even trying?*

But the reason you do the work is to combat exactly this sort of moment. I'm not going to pretend it was easy, or quick. But I was able to do the work from these pages on myself. I was able to take an honest inventory of where I was and what I was feeling. I matched it against my values and my purpose. And I came out the other side more determined than ever. Because I realized that I wanted to live my life in a way that would have made my daughter proud that I was her father. Instead of giving in to the habits I had developed to avoid my pain, I had to work out how to integrate them into who I was now. That journey will never be complete. It is work I will have to do the rest of my life. But I believe I will be ultimately stronger because of it. I may process emotion differently, but even that was an advantage. Because that extra step of distance allowed me to take a look at what was happening and analyse it.

Mike Tyson's memorable quote is more relevant than ever here: 'Everyone has a plan until they get punched in the face.' For all of us, it is how we respond to bumps in the road that defines our journey. You can plan all you want, you can set the best of intentions, but it's when times get tough that you really find out who you are. I believe that being hit in the face and getting up benefits you more than any number of sunny days when you manage to do everything perfectly.

The first thing to say is to seek professional help. If you have received a body blow, you need to get a medic in your corner. It's as simple as that. This book doesn't know your exact story, so it can't give you specific advice in that regard. But if you are really struggling, talk to your doctor or a trusted medical professional. Don't try to fix yourself. I need to remind you that nothing in this book is a replacement for expert medical care. This is non-negotiable.

The Serenity Prayer

After every Alcoholics Anonymous or Narcotics Anonymous meeting, we all hold hands and say the Serenity Prayer, and it's got nothing to do with religion if that's not your thing. It's a roadmap for acceptance when life gets tough. 'Grant me the serenity to accept the things I cannot change, the courage to change the things I can, and the wisdom to know the difference.' Let that sink in. Acceptance isn't waving the white flag; it's about facing what you're up against. It's about not wasting energy on what you can't control and laser-focusing on what you can. The courage to change is about getting your hands dirty, whether breaking a bad habit, walking away from a toxic relationship, or staring down a fear. And wisdom? That's knowing when to fight and when to let it go. Understanding what things you can change and what things you can't. Once you find the silver lining, you won't regret anything you've done, and you'll be grateful for everything that happens for you – the good and the bad.

Radical Gratitude

Dr John Demartini, who I mentioned earlier, has inspired millions to transform their lives through the power of gratitude, and teaches the importance of finding gratitude in every experience. He says: 'Anything you can't say thank you for is baggage; anything you can say thank you for is fuel.' One of the key exercises Dr Demartini promotes is to rewrite your story by finding the worst thing that has ever happened to you and writing 100 reasons why you are grateful for it. This exercise is designed to shift your perspective and uncover the hidden benefits and growth opportunities within your challenges. Try it: think about the most difficult or painful experience in your life. Consider how this event has shaped who you are today, and then list 100 reasons why you are grateful for the experience. Many people have made profound life changes after doing this exercise, because it fundamentally changes their perspective on the situation and how they perceive it. Like focusing on the white space around the black dot.

To put it simply, perspective is about choosing to see things differently or focusing on certain areas rather than others. I hate to admit it, but it's quite like the expression 'Come on, it could be worse!' Now, although this can completely invalidate people's emotions and leave them feeling worse, the truth is: it could be worse! Most people experience first-world problems but look at them through a distorted lens. If only they could zoom out and realize that the things we usually worry about aren't as bad as we think they are. As the saying goes: 'If it's not going to matter in five years, it's not worth spending five minutes thinking about.' That's true. Worrying about the small stuff only leaves us feeling worse, and in the end it doesn't really matter.

When we practise radical gratitude, there cannot be a purely bad experience. Because within it, there is something that we can learn. Now, I'm not here to tell you that all experiences are fun. They sting, bruise, and can leave you feeling like you want to press the 'fuck it' button and do nothing but lie in bed and zone out in front of the TV to distract you from everyone and everything. But once you've had your moment to call the universe every name under the sun, you can learn to take a step back, breathe and ask yourself: *What's the silver lining here?* Trust me, it might seem impossible now, but with practice, there's always one there.

You can apply this even to the most difficult of circumstances. For example, the worst break-up in the world, the one where it's like someone has pressed stop on your favourite song, leaving you stranded in silence, trying to hum along to a tune you can't quite remember. That can be an opportunity to understand why you needed that relationship so much. What was it giving you that you can learn to generate from within? And consider the fact that you allowed yourself to love so deeply. That's an experience that you will not ultimately regret. To be someone who has the capacity to experience that strength of feeling, can you come to see that as a positive thing? Think about how many people must move through life never experiencing that profound intensity of connection. But you have, and there can be gratitude in that.

Or maybe this break-up can function as a wake-up call, the line in the sand, the reset button. The bottom of the swimming pool that you kick back up from to the surface. What are your dreams, the ones that got sidelined? What have you always wanted to explore? Now's the time. Healing isn't linear. Some days you'll feel on top of the world, ready to seize new adventures, and on others, well, you might just want to pull the covers over your head. Both are okay. Be gentle with yourself. Allow yourself the grace to feel, to grieve, and to gradually let go. Surround yourself with loved ones – anchors that remind you of your worth and the love that still surrounds you, even in the absence of that one person.

There is beauty in realizing that the universe, in its infinite wisdom, often removes what's familiar to make space for what's even more aligned with our journey. While it's hard to imagine now, there are experiences, connections and adventures waiting just around the corner, that are tailor-made for the person you're becoming. While the pain is real, so is the promise of new beginnings. So, when you're ready, embrace the journey ahead, knowing that every ending is but a prelude to a new chapter.

Losing your job might feel like the end of the world, until you see it as the chance to finally launch that business you've been dreaming about. Some of the world's most successful businesses were born after one or even multiple failures. Some founders lost their career or started the business merely for survival, and their struggles became the bedrock of their later success.

A health scare might be a wake-up call and become a chance to focus on what really matters, whether that's slowing down, prioritizing your wellness or appreciating the little things in life.

Often the hardest moments are the ones that push you to rebuild a stronger version of yourself. The most powerful example of radical gratitude I've ever come across is from my best friend and business partner, Liam. One day, Liam received a phone call that would change his life for ever. His dad, his best mate, his role model – the man who lit up every room with jokes and laughter – had taken his own life by stepping in front of a train. At first, Liam was convinced it had to be a mistake. His dad had been so full of life, the last person anyone would expect to do that. But after going to the morgue and having to identify his hand – the only part that was left to show him – as soon as he saw it, the harsh reality set in. It was true.

Understandably, he was devastated. But in the months and years that followed, Liam didn't just survive, he rebuilt and thrived. He found happiness again. He had two beautiful children, and became one of the most grounded and grateful people I've ever met. But how? One day, I asked him: 'Liam, how do you manage to stay so positive after something like that?' He told me that every now and then, when the grief creeps back in, when he starts missing his dad and spiralling into questions that don't have answers, he takes himself to a quiet space. Just a few minutes alone. And in those moments, he closes his eyes and does something most people would never think to do. He imagines something far worse. He pictures losing everything he has now – his wife, his children, his health – and he prays to be back in a scenario where it's only his dad that he has lost. It's brutal, and of course it's painful, but he says that in doing this, when he opens his eyes and is reminded of what he *does* have, he is met with a rush of gratitude. Not because the pain disappears, but because he's shifted his focus back to the blessings in front of him.

Now, this kind of technique is intense, and Liam has a level of mental resilience and self-awareness that makes it work for him. It's not something I'd recommend without the right support or guidance. But it demonstrates something important: when life throws us the harshest of experiences, it's not the end, and we can use radical tools to find our way back.

Hopefully the situations you're facing don't mean you have to go this deep, but even a subtle shift in perspective can be enough to spark a little light when things feel dark. Sometimes surviving is the goal. But when you also learn how to sit with the pain, process it and reframe it, that's where you can not only survive but grow through it, too. That's the power of radical gratitude.

Be Suspicious of No

There was a film that came out when I was a teenager called *Yes Man*. In it, Jim Carrey plays a guy who has become entirely negative about his life after getting divorced. He goes to a self-help seminar where he is convinced to say yes to every opportunity that comes in front of him. Of course, it's Jim Carrey, so this leads to a whole lot of funny absurd stuff happening and in the end he gets the girl.

Now, I definitely don't think you should say yes to everything. But I do think you should be suspicious of no. Because when we are in a difficult place, very often the first things to go are our curiosity and confidence. The problem is that's exactly the time when we need new ideas, new things and new experiences. Because the old ones haven't worked out.

Let's think again about a break-up. When you went through your first heartbreak, what was the advice you were given? There are plenty more fish in the sea? At the time that felt like the worst advice ever. But as you get older, have you ever noticed that, actually, the best way of getting over a break-up is meeting someone new? There's a scientific reason for this. When we can't stop thinking about someone, even though it makes us feel bad, we are trapped in those old connections our brain has made, and we are reinforcing them. When we meet someone new, our brain literally makes new connections. We aren't stuck in that cycle any more. It's the same when we're trying to bounce back from any setback. There is the temptation to hold off on anything new until after you're out the other side – to say no to human connection, to experiences and opportunities at exactly the moment they could most benefit you.

So don't always say yes. But be suspicious of no.

We're Stronger When We're Connected

I don't care how tough you think you are, if you're doing life completely solo, you're vulnerable. Full stop. Not in the 'vulnerability is a superpower way' we spoke about earlier. Life is full of contradictions, and isolation is a vulnerability that is the complete opposite. It's not a power, it's disempowering.

Think of it like this: imagine a phone with no signal. Useless, right? Doesn't matter how new the model is, how much it cost or how many features it has, if it's not connected to anything, it can't reach anyone, it can't load anything, and it can't do shit. But put it on a network, and suddenly it becomes powerful. It can stream, connect, call, create, move money, run a business. Why? Because it's plugged into something bigger than itself. When we're isolated, we're just high-potential humans with no bandwidth. No connection, no momentum, no real impact. But when we're connected to the right people, the right energy, the right mission, we're a whole system. We amplify each other. We plug into shared power.

However, just like your phone needs a good signal, you need the *right* people. Not just anyone. If you're surrounded by energy drainers, doubters, or people playing small, it's like having full bars but being on the wrong network – nothing flows properly. You've got to find the tribe that charges you, supports you, calls you out and lifts you up.

Finding Your Tribe

The right bunch are people in your life who support you and allow you to be you. You should feel confident that they have your best interests at heart. You should look forward to seeing them. They should feel happy for you when things go well and commiserate with you when things go badly. They should spur you on, helping you to remain motivated, and increase your confidence. They should be people whose advice you would listen to. Who offer a different perspective when they share their own experiences and coping strategies. But they should keep you honest too. They should be willing to challenge you and hold you accountable if they think you need it. If they share the same values and goals that you do, you reinforce each other's commitment to those values and goals.

Now, obviously not every single person in your life is going to tick every box. You might have friends you love but who give terrible life advice. Or friends that you have very specific relationships with. But surrounding yourself with enough of the right people is absolutely key to dealing with setbacks. Have you heard the saying 'You become the sum of the five people you spend the most time with'? I really believe it's true. There have been studies that show that negativity can literally be contagious. If we surround ourselves with people who push us to try new things, to grow and learn and develop, to live passionate and authentic lives, they lift us up. If we surround ourselves with people who roll their eyes, who are threatened by new experiences and mock trying at life, then they will drag us down.

At The Coaching Masters, we've seen first-hand how powerful it can be to find your tribe. Our community isn't just a collection of people. It's a family. When you're surrounded by others who share your goals and values, it gives you a sense of belonging, which is one of our strongest instinctual desires. It's not just about having people cheer you on – though that's a big part of it – it's about being in an environment where growth is the norm. You feel like you can be the person you are meant to be, where challenges are met head-on, and where every win, no matter how small, is celebrated. And the impact? It's life-changing. We've had members start businesses together, collaborate on projects they never would have dreamed of tackling alone, and even build relationships that go far beyond business. We're talking about people who met in our community, fell in love and started families. That's the power of finding your tribe – incredible things happen when you meet your people. So, if you're feeling stuck or your motivation feels low, take a look at who you're spending your time with. Are they lifting you up or dragging you down? And when you find your tribe, the ones who truly get you, that's when the magic happens.

Zero-Sum Thinking

This is a mindset trap where you believe that there is a finite amount of success or happiness in the world, and that someone else getting it reduces your chances of attaining it. It is the ultimate fixed mindset. Relationships with people who fall into this trap are defined by competition, conflict and scorekeeping. Often you come away from seeing them with decreased energy and motivation. If there are people in your life who make you feel like this, I would think very carefully about the impact they are having on you. If you have multiple people like this in your circle, I would make a real effort to balance them out with others or consider removing them from your circle entirely. That little voice in your head saying you've got enough friends and you don't need to make any more? Remember that's your brain trying to keep you safe by stopping you from experiencing new things. By now you know what to do when that happens.

Let's do a quick thought experiment. Imagine something

really good has just happened to you. Let's say it's connected to your professional life. Do you have people in your circle who you would feel confident telling and people you wouldn't? There's a good chance the people you wouldn't tell are suffering from zero-sum thinking.

Shout Your Wins

Remember to celebrate your achievements, no matter how small. This isn't just a nice idea; it's essential to keeping your momentum going. When you pause to acknowledge your wins, you reinforce the behaviours that are driving your success. If you don't acknowledge them, they mean less to your brain. Whether it's finally wrapping up that beast of a project at work or smashing a personal best at the gym, these victories deserve to be celebrated. So go ahead, treat yourself to that nice dinner, share your success with friends who will genuinely hype you up, or just take a moment to soak in the satisfaction of a job well done.

Don't wait for permission either. Too many people stay quiet because they're scared of coming across as arrogant or 'too much'. But here's the truth – the world is already full of people shrinking themselves. We don't need more of that. We need more people who are willing to own their progress, out loud.

And sharing your wins doesn't just boost your own motivation, it also shows others what's possible. You never know who's watching, silently struggling, just waiting for proof that it *can* be done. Be that proof. Celebrate, not just for yourself, but to create a ripple effect for everyone else who needs to see that someone like them is doing it too. By celebrating your wins, you give them permission to celebrate theirs as well.

Quality Not Quantity

You don't need to have a massive social circle of fifty people. It's better to have a small number of the right people. You can be more intentional about who you surround yourself with. If 95 per cent of the people you hang around with are people who went to the same school as you when you were fourteen, then you might want to think about widening that pool a little. There's absolutely nothing wrong with deep, old friendships. But exclusively spending time with very old friends can be limiting. People change, friendships change, and that's absolutely fine and normal.

As our self-esteem and self-worth rise, the need to cling to anyone who will have us lessens and we can be much more deliberate about who we spend time with – and hey, if you can find a community like ours and have quality and quantity at the same time then that's even better.

Clean Your Socials

Remember that you don't have to be directly in contact with someone for them to influence you. Make sure that your social feeds, podcast choices and reading lists are putting you in touch with the best, most inspiring ideas. Negativity can be spread online too. If there is someone you follow whose posts make you feel bad, stop following them. Seek inspiration from those you admire – the ones who have achieved what you aspire to. Follow them on social media, read their books, take their courses, absorb their wisdom, and use them as inspiration. Let their positive mindset rub off on you.

And don't be afraid to go a step further and *block* people.

I mean it. In today's world, your online environment is just as important as your physical one. It doesn't take much – a single snarky comment or a passive dig in your inbox can throw off your energy for hours. I've had it happen loads of times. In the early days I'd fire something back, thinking I was standing my ground, but honestly it just made things worse. Their words festered. Lived rent-free in my head. Distracted me from the things that actually mattered.

Now? I don't hesitate. The second I see something that feels even remotely off, I don't even finish reading it, I don't argue, I don't overthink – I just block, delete, move on. Simple. No drama. No explanation needed. They don't have the right to sit in your virtual space if they're taking from it. You've got billions of people out there to choose from, so be picky about who you let into your digital world. Protect your energy like it's one of your most valuable assets, because in today's digital era it is.

Everyone is Going through Something

When we are honest and authentic about what we're going through, we open up a space for other people to feel too. I posted about the loss of our baby, and was astonished by the number of people who replied and thanked me because it had happened to them and nobody talks about it. We don't deal with setbacks by pretending they never happened. We deal with setbacks by looking them in the eye, and by showing honesty and compassion in our relationships with others.

Think of how often in life you are annoyed by someone. They might bash a supermarket trolley into your ankles without apologizing, cut you off in traffic, or steal your milk from the work fridge. Take a moment to think about what they might be going through. An ill parent, a troubled child, a bad break-up. Imagine how hard they are finding life. Now think again about what they did. It doesn't seem such a big deal now, does it.

There was a time where my usual coach-like positive energy became distant, and I would have seemed snappy. Not because I got a kick from giving out toxic energy, but because I was going through something myself and dealing with the loss of our baby.

But after the rough times can quickly follow the smooth. In September 2023, for the first time in my life, I cried tears of joy, as I held my son in my arms. He had been born on exactly the same day of the year as his sister, Mia, who had been born sleeping exactly two years before.

I was told there's a name for the baby you have after such a loss – a 'rainbow baby'. It symbolizes the light that comes after the storm; the beauty and hope that can push through, even in the darkest moments. We named him Ocean because it felt right. His name reflects the balance between two forces. From me, he gets the ocean's relentless, powerful, unstoppable drive. From Dayana, he has the calm, peaceful depth of the sea – the kind of stillness that makes you feel grounded. Together, those forces make him who he is. And that's the balance I hope you'll find in your life, too. The strength to face life head-on, but with the calmness to ride the waves when things get rough.

Unfortunately, in 2024, Dayana and I made the decision to separate. She is now based with her family in the US, where I cannot visit because of my criminal record. Despite the highs and lows and the roller-coaster of life, I can genuinely say that I am very grateful for the time I had with such an amazing woman – and for our beautiful baby boy. I look forward to spending the rest of my life connected to her, maybe in a different way than I'd imagined, but still in a relationship that I'm truly grateful for. Ocean, if you ever read this book: your mum and I love you so much. And Mia, if you get this message, we both love you so much too.

Because life isn't a movie. You don't ever roll the end credits. It keeps going. Remember the caption my friend put in front of those two photos of me in front of the courthouse? 'Nothing Changes.' I know now just how wrong that is. Everything changes. And that is where all of the pain and beauty of life come from. Don't waste your time chasing a happy ending, because the camera is still rolling. For now, live in the only place that matters. Because as long as you keep going, as long as you keep striving, as long as you keep doing the work and turning your adversity into assets, there will always be the opportunity for more chapters of your story to reveal themselves.

If there's one thing to take from this story it's that adversity isn't just an obstacle, it's an opportunity. It's life's way of forcing us to grow. Yeah, it hurts, but it also makes our stories worth telling. So, the next time it feels like the world is bearing down on you, remember this: you're exactly where you're supposed to be. This is your process of becoming the person you're meant to be. Your journey, your story. It's not just happening to you, it's happening *for* you. And through you, it's happening for others, too.

Key Takeaways

- Practise gratitude and every setback will only ever be temporary.
- It is how we deal with the rainstorms, not how we enjoy the sunny days, that defines our lives. It's not about how hard we punch, but how we deal with being punched.

- We are stronger when we're together. Find your tribe and make sure they are the people that are going to lift you up, not drag you down.
- Remember to apply this rule to your online relationships as well as your real-life ones. In today's world, we have the capacity to reach billions of people who can support you in ways your physical proximity never could.

CHAPTER 10

Becoming Unlimited

'The plan is for the documentary to be called . . . *The Psychopath Life Coach.'*

'Jesus.' As I sit there, listening to them describe what is going to go into the documentary, I feel the old familiar darkness around me. It is *not* going to be a flattering piece. It is going to detail my criminal, violent past. They are going to speak to my mother, to my teachers, to people I hung around with in those days. It will also give voice to accusations that I am leading a cult. As ever, I hear that little voice: 'Of course. How did you think this wouldn't happen, you buffoon?'

The thought of my past being dragged out and displayed in front of the world just felt risky. My first thought was how it might harm The Coaching Masters community. Would people want to be associated with 'the psychopath life coach'?! I knew that we were doing good and helping people, and the thought of all that coming crashing down just felt so uncertain.

I didn't get much sleep that night. But when I woke up, I focused on how I could move forward as the truest version of myself. I called my trusted circle and told them what I was going to do. I was going to go all out to support the documentary. Because when every single thing that could be bad about it was viewed from a different angle, it could be seen as a massive positive. Instead of the world seeing a monster, what if they saw a flawed and vulnerable human being? What if, instead of focusing on the bad things I had done, they saw my determination not to let that define me – and recognized my passion for helping other people? I had used my story to inspire thousands of people around the world. But this documentary could reach millions. If even a tiny percentage of them saw what I was trying to do and joined The Coaching Masters community, then the ripples out into the world would be incredible.

I realized it was another step towards being vulnerable – connecting with people on a deeper level and uncovering the parts of myself I still kept hidden away. I decided to become involved as much as possible, volunteering my time to the project in any way I could. I was interviewed, did media to promote it, and I told everyone to watch it and even hosted a premiere at a cinema in Mayfair – which was full to the brim, with a red carpet, celebrities, paparazzi. The whole shebang.

It made me think that it was a sliding door moment – everyone was there either to watch my collapse as my brutal honesty hit the world screens, or witness history, in the form of one of the most unique documentaries that would impact lives in a way others would never have dared to.

When it aired on Netflix, the documentary hit the top-ten charts within the first week, drove millions in sales – and, most importantly, connected me with people on a whole new level. People didn't just see my mistakes. They saw the transform-ation, the journey, and the impact that I'd made and that others were inspired to make too. I received messages from people in all walks of life saying they had never connected with anybody like they had with me. I mean, 1 per cent of the population are psychopaths, but about 0 per cent are brave enough to speak up about it – and I am proud that I took the risk. It paid off in more ways than I could have imagined.

Of course, there were a few haters, but I knew how to handle them – and to be honest, the main complaint was that it was *too* positive. I couldn't help but smile at that. I think they wanted to see me kill somebody or something. Well, there I was again, proving them wrong.

An interesting moment popped up during an interview after the documentary was released. Someone asked me: what does 'buffoon' actually mean? And then I realized. I didn't really know. How wild is that? Just from the way my dad had said it, I knew it was really bad. I'd mixed it up in my mind with 'baboon', and I figured it meant some kind of idiotic clown. But then I finally looked it up. It turns out that I wasn't miles off, but I wasn't exactly on target either. According to the *Oxford English Dictionary*, a buffoon is 'a ridiculous but amusing person'. The word that once crushed me, boxed me in, and made me feel small and worthless was literally defined as ridiculous – and amusing. In that moment, the word no longer weighed me down. Ridiculous but amusing. I could live with that.

I'm not a hero or a villain. A saint or a monster. I'm me. I'm still learning and I'm still growing. Still trying to do better.

I used to believe I was stupid – fully, completely convinced. It wasn't a passing thought but a deep, unshakable belief. And yet, here I am now, looking back and realizing how wrong I was. The truth is, I was never stupid. But do you know what was stupid? Not trying, not pushing myself, not going after the things I wanted in life – that was what was really stupid. I was letting my own mind hold me back from everything I was capable of the whole time.

I hope my story inspires you to see just how much you're capable of. For years, I let the stories in my head control me. They were built from pain, fear and the opinions of others. When I changed those stories, I changed my life. I saw that I wasn't any of those things I'd believed I was. I am enough. I am worthy. I am lovable. And so are you.

Each of us has the capacity to change, to transform our lives and the lives of those around us. We're not doomed to be trapped by our past or shackled by who we once were. We're not just products of our environment or our circumstances. We have the power to choose, to design the kind of people we want to be, to become the architects of our own lives. And when you get that, when you really get that, you can use it not just to better yourself but to make the world a better place.

You know me well enough by now to realize there is no neat bow after this moment. No perfect ending. To be honest, when all the surface-level success fades away, can I say I'm left with an unshakable sense of self-worth and love? Not yet. Is it my personality disorder or am I still on my journey? I don't know. But I know every step I take brings me closer to that place.

Like the message in this book, I know my growth isn't a destination; it's a journey. It's unlimited.

If you're still wondering exactly what it means to become unlimited, let me share a story with you called 'The Rice and Chessboard'. In it, a wise man invents the game of chess and shows it to the emperor. The emperor is so impressed by the game that he asks what reward the man would like. The inventor, who is also a mathematician, asks for a simple reward: one grain of rice on the first square, then double on every subsequent square. 1, 2, 4, 8, 16 and so on. Thinking this seems like no reward at all, the emperor, who is not a mathematician, agrees. Using this rule though, the total amount of rice due after 64 doublings is 18,446,744,073,709,551,615 (eighteen quintillion, four hundred and forty-six quadrillion, seven hundred and forty-four trillion, seventy-three billion, seven hundred and nine million, five hundred and fifty-one thousand, six hundred and fifteen). This is because of something called 'exponential growth'.

Personal development, business, life, and you as an individual all have the ability for exponential growth. That might sound like a technical term, but it's basically like a snowball rolling downhill. At first, the snowball starts small and rolls slowly, but as it continues on, it picks up speed and size, growing faster and bigger, and before you know it, it's huge! That's exponential growth: small, consistent efforts that seem slow at first but eventually explode into massive progress.

Imagine plotting it on a graph. The line starts flat, steady, almost unnoticeable, but then it begins to curve upward, accelerating rapidly. It's what separates those stuck in linear growth, steady and slow, from those who know how to compound their efforts for massive results. By reading this book and applying each chapter to your own life, you will start to create this kind of growth in any area you choose.

That's the closest I can get to a scientific explanation of what it means to be unlimited. Once you hit that 'uptick', you'll be blown away by where it takes you.

The point is, no matter where you started or what you've been through, you've got the power to turn your life into a force for good. So don't let your adversities define you. Because you, like me, can turn adversity into an asset and your life into something that matters. And when you do that, you'll find that the world isn't just a better place for you, it's a better place because of you. That, my friends, is the power of becoming unlimited.

If you're wondering if you can become unlimited yourself, let me remind you of the words that changed my life for ever. My prison tutor, Suzie, who looked me straight in the eye and said: 'Of course you can . . .'

I'm now saying the same to you: *OF COURSE YOU CAN!*

Because you are ready and willing to do the work. You know you want to change and you know how to do it. You're looking at an honest reflection of yourself. You recognize the subconscious stories your brain is telling you. But you know that you can literally change your mind and your reality. You know how to find your deepest motivations and values and tap into them to live with fierce purpose. You know how to face your fears and make your peace with discomfort. You have learned how to integrate, and not repress the parts of yourself that society sees as less desirable. You can live with radical authenticity. You move through the universe with raw imperfect action. You know how to trick your triggers so that you do more of the things you want to and less of the things you don't. You are a source of kind acts, not through selflessness but through self-fulness, receiving all of the many benefits that come to us when we do things for other people. And you know how to achieve all of this, despite all the setbacks you may face.

This isn't just the end of a book, it's the beginning of a new chapter in your life. From here, the path is yours to create. You know what's possible, and you have everything you need to make it happen.

The question isn't 'Can you do it?' You already know the answer to that. The question is 'What will you do?'

You've heard the stories, you've understood the lessons, and now it's your turn to step into the real you – the version of yourself that's always been there, waiting for this moment. Take everything you've learned here and make it count. Because the crazy thing about this thing we call life is that you never know what's coming – and if you've listened carefully to what I've shared in this book, you know your best days are yet to come.

So, go out there and show the world what happens when someone decides to break free from limits.

Remember that black dot?

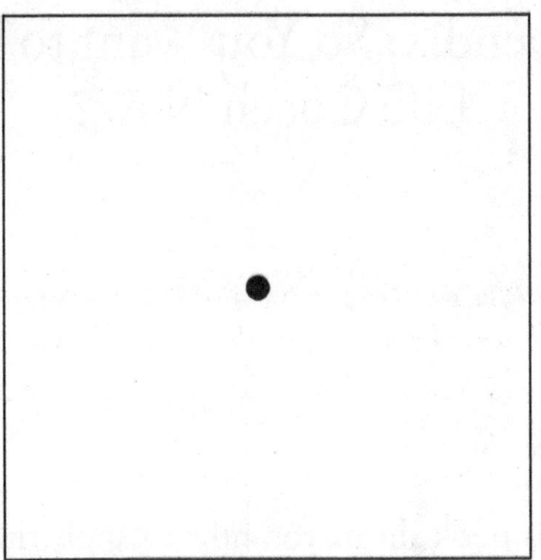

Can you now see how much white space there is around it?

You should now understand that the possibilities for you are infinite.

Just remember . . .

You are not your past. You are not your mistakes. You are not your flaws.

You are *unlimited*.

Appendix: So You Want to be a
Life Coach Now?

A bonus section for aspiring coaches: if this book has sparked your interest in helping others and possibly turning your own adversity into a coaching career, the following pages provide a starter kit to help you begin.

Although this book shows you how to apply the world-class tools we have developed at The Coaching Masters to yourself, you may well be interested in taking the journey into becoming a life coach. So here I've included the method we teach known as 'The 6 As'.

This is for those of you who want to embody everything you've learned in this book and turn it into a career. Below you'll find a simple introduction to coaching business strategy. Of course, there is more technology today with AI and all sorts of other amazing things at your disposal, but this strategy is timeless – it's the same strategy I used to make a six-figure income in under a year. It will allow you to understand how close you may be to impacting countless lives, including your own, by running your own freedom-based and passion-led online business with unlimited potential – and how you can turn your adversities into literal tangible financial assets.

1. Accreditation

Of course, as a leader in the coach training world, I would always recommend you get the best possible training in knowing how to coach people. As explained previously, coaching isn't all about sharing your personal experiences but also about using tangible tools, techniques, models and frameworks to help people break down limiting beliefs, push through fear, find their purpose, and know how to question and challenge others in any subject area they're passionate about. It's also vital you build the confidence needed to coach people, and there is no better way of doing this than in a learning environment. During our coaching accreditation course, you get a chance to practise your coaching with other coaches in live online workshop environments – as well as learn the theory throughout the course. Our courses also grant you the ability to become a member of the International Coaching Federation, boosting your authority and your trust and value as a coach. It won't take you years to get started either, as this is not a regulated industry that means you have to go back to college or university. You can be qualified in as little as twelve weeks, and you can start learning without any previous experience or qualifications.

The best part is that, when you train to become a coach, you become your first client. You can't help but apply what you learn to yourself – and the practice and feedback you get from the training mean you will completely transform your own life through the process. Not bad for a by-product of learning a highly valuable, income-generating skill that will help make the world a better place, right?

2. Accuracy

'I can help everyone. I'm going to change the world!' That was my proud declaration to a marketing consultant soon after I embarked on my coaching journey. At that stage, I wasn't even sure if 'coach' was the right word; I was calling myself a 'personal development mentor'.

The consultant's sceptical reaction didn't deter me. Fired up, I reached out to people everywhere. And voilà, my first client! They paid me £600 for a twelve-week programme. I was ecstatic. But that thrill was short-lived. While I managed to coach a variety of individuals, from single mums to struggling students, I battled with pricing and felt my confidence wane. Worse yet, the transformative results I aimed for seemed elusive, and my passion for coaching dimmed. In search of a solution, I convinced myself a flashy website was the answer. Overwhelmed by options, a site designed specifically for coaches caught my attention. The testimonials, design and messaging spoke directly to me.

That moment highlighted the power of a niche. Reflecting on my journey, I realized that my true strength lay in mindset coaching. So I rebranded and immersed myself in this specialty. The result? My client list grew, and their transformations were profound. But a deeper realization awaited me. It wasn't just about mindset; it was about the kind of people I resonated with most: entrepreneurs. Their drive, passion and zest mirrored mine.

After embracing this niche – a mindset coach for entrepreneurs – everything changed for me. Understanding your niche goes beyond the surface. It's about knowing the specific problems you can solve, the dreams you will help realize. It's about instilling confidence in potential clients that you are their best choice.

Seeking to cater to everyone can lead to serving no one effectively. Think of restaurants that offer everything. They attract those who are undecided about what they want, often compromising on quality. But if you had a craving for, say, authentic Chinese, wouldn't you prefer a specialist? The same goes for coaching. Specializing doesn't limit your skills; it sharpens them, focusing them on delivering the best in one area.

Many people have this belief that they're different, thinking solutions work for others but not for them. This mindset, often rooted in past disappointments, sets them apart. Your messaging needs to speak directly to them, assuring them that your coaching is tailored to their unique needs. This personalized touch fosters trust and confidence, making them more likely to invest in your services.

If you're without a niche, understanding your client's needs can become elusive. Triggering, isn't it? Let's look at it this way: a fresh graduate at twenty-one, aiming for career confidence, is worlds apart from a 55-year-old woman, post-menopause, seeking deeper self-understanding. The age-old saying 'If you try to please everybody, you end up pleasing nobody' rings truer than ever. It's not just about your coaching style; it's about zeroing in on the individual you're coaching. Recognize this: no one can understand everybody. But once you zone in on a specific demographic, you can truly connect with their psyche.

Imagine hopping on a sales call and instantly grasping the person on the other end of the line's innermost fears and current pain points. That's the insight you'll gain from repeated interactions with a certain group.

What about knowing your ideal client's aspirations inside out? Take a millennial entrepreneur, for instance. They might value travel, societal impact or the thrill of success. Their nightmares? Probably being branded a failure, facing rejection or the dread of mediocrity. Their hurdles might include focus or self-belief. But that's just a quick snapshot, and every client group has its unique narrative.

Navigating Niche Worries

Doubts creeping in? 'What if my chosen niche falls flat – or worse, I loathe it?' Relax. If you've chosen with care, the chances of connecting with your audience increase tenfold. But what if it all goes south? Simply pivot. Adjust your profile a bit and refocus on a new area that feels more aligned. Give it a solid try, a few months at least, before reconsidering. It's human to second-guess once you've settled on a niche.

I recall a client ready to swap her niche in coaching professional men as she was convinced men were too indecisive. With a gentle nudge from me, she persevered and through some communication development soon had her clients nodding in agreement as they started working with her. She's now thriving and relishing her niche that she almost gave up on.

Rapid Expertise in Coaching

Here's a gem: you can quickly become an expert. Consuming three books on a topic instantly puts you ahead of the curve. Committing to one book a month for a mere five years catapults you among the world's top 1 per cent of experts. Most dabble in general knowledge; few hone in on mastering a subject. Consider the film *Catch Me If You Can*. Based on real events, it chronicles the audacious ventures of Frank William Abagnale, a young man with an uncanny ability to impersonate professionals. He didn't just masquerade as any professional – he convincingly played an airline pilot, breezed through corridors as a doctor, and defended cases as a lawyer. Yet one of his most astonishing feats was as a university lecturer. At the tender age of seventeen, without any legitimate qualifications, he taught a full university course. His secret to staying ahead? He admitted, 'I just read one chapter ahead of the rest of the class.' The beauty of this tale is the realization that to guide, mentor or teach, you don't need to be miles ahead; just a step or two can make all the difference. Combine this with powerful coaching questions and strategies and you have a recipe to change lives, profoundly.

3. Awareness

So, you've laid the groundwork, you've defined your ideal client, and now comes the real work: making sure your ideal client knows you're out there. I'll level with you here: it doesn't matter if you're the best coach. If people don't know you exist, you're like a masterpiece painting hidden in an attic. I've seen genius coaches with just a handful of clients, not because they lack skills but because they remain hidden gems. Not broadcasting your value to a wide audience ensures one thing: your transformative coaching won't get the chance to make a difference, either in people's lives or in your bank account.

Your Virtual Room

Think of your online presence as a big seminar hall. If you're hosting an event with the intention to sell something, it's imperative that the hall is filled with interested attendees. Imagine trying to sell financial planning to a room full of toddlers. Cute, but pointless, right? Your social media platforms are no different.

If your digital 'room' is crowded with old friends, distant relatives, and that couple you met on that 2009 cruise, sales will be a challenge. Sure, a handful might engage out of loyalty or curiosity, but for sustainable success, your audience must align with your niche.

It's easy to fall into a trap, especially when you are new to coaching. The rosy vision of clients flooding in just because you hung out your digital shingle is tempting. Bursting that bubble might hurt a bit, but here's the silver lining: instead of waiting for clients, why not create opportunities?

Harnessing Social Networking

Social media isn't just for holiday snaps and cat videos any more. It's evolved into a powerful, global networking tool, facilitating everything from business ventures to personal connections. If you're thinking, *Oh, I just use it to check on friends*, it's time to pivot. Networking is the name of the game now. But despite the power of this tool, many still resist its pull.

Pushing past these reservations is vital. The approach is straightforward: identify potential clients and engage with them. Find them, connect, and invite them into your sphere. In practical terms? Friend requests on Facebook, follows on Instagram, and connections on LinkedIn. Social media is full of groups and communities that will mirror your niche. Find them and engage consistently. For instance, if your niche is at the intersection of entrepreneurship and mindset, joining a Facebook group dedicated to entrepreneurial mindset could be a gold mine. Engage, connect, and gradually your ideal audience will grow, eager to see what you have to offer.

4. Attraction

You've identified your unique positioning and built a social media account with a few hundred ideal clients. What comes next is essential: magnetizing these individuals towards forming a meaningful relationship with you. Because, let's face it, when people trust, like and feel understood by you, they're more likely to want to work with you. To forge this bond, consider your audience more like potential friends than mere followers. One powerful tool at your disposal? Social media content. But it's not about simply uploading; it's about resonating.

Crafting Connection through Content

Aware of your audience's nuances, tailor your content to their wavelength. Share relatable stories, offer helpful strategies, and even use phrases they're familiar with. Picture this: if you cater to professional women in their forties seeking motivation, a post that empathizes with their work–life balance while offering tips to improve productivity would hit home. You've stepped into their shoes and are speaking their language. This establishes you as not only knowledgeable but also empathetic, drawing them to your offerings.

Consider this. What narratives can illuminate your potential clients' challenges and inspire action? How can you position yourself as the answer they've been seeking? It's through insightful content that these realizations dawn upon them. Venturing into content creation might feel daunting. There could be apprehensions about perceptions, possible rejections, or even ridicule. As you wade into unfamiliar waters, remember that these feelings are normal. Yet the rewards far outweigh the discomfort. Sharing impactful content not only carves out a unique online niche for you but also draws clients straight to your doorstep.

A Glimpse into Authenticity

Sharing slices of your personal life infuses your online presence with authenticity. This vulnerability fosters trust, making your audience see you beyond the coach facade. It's not always about the hard sell. Sometimes, it's just about showing up and letting them into your world. As they resonate with your personal shares and online content, they're drawn to your services not because of aggressive marketing but because of genuine alignment.

Consider platforms like Facebook: users connect as 'friends'. By sharing content, you're not just engaging with existing connections but also branching out to potential ones. This mutual interaction lays the groundwork for future collaborations. And as the saying goes, people buy from those they trust. Sometimes, a simple snapshot from your life can pique interest, leading curious viewers down the rabbit hole of your services.

What makes you memorable isn't always business-related. It could be the humour you bring to the table or even the candid moments you share. Being at the forefront of their mind, however, is the goal.

Endless Possibilities with Content

The brilliance of content lies in its expansive reach and versatility. In contrast to traditional media, which might burn a hole in your pocket, social media content is free. You're unrestricted, with the liberty to share as you please. It can also be rehashed in books, courses, blogs and quotes, providing continuous value and visibility. Remember, while print media has a short lifespan, online content remains searchable, evergreen, and a potential lead generator for life. The equation is simple: valuable content equals sales. Whether your primary drive is financial or you're fuelled by passion, social media content is your pathway to inspire others and to personal success.

5. Authority

Becoming a six-figure coach and surging beyond this demands more than just skill – it necessitates being recognized as an authority in your field. To convince your clients that you can elevate them to a better life, you must radiate authority. After all, at the heart of most aspirations, like money, power and success, lies the pursuit of elevated status. This elevation is both external, in terms of societal recognition, and internal, as self-worth. Clients look to you not just for tools or techniques, but for transformation. They want to believe you can help them transcend their current realities.

Surprisingly, it's not just about the value you provide; it's also about the aura you exude. Clients yearn for a coach who exudes a sense of confidence, empowerment and assurance. Achieving that aura means building your authority. To kick-start that journey, consider the following authority-boosting strategies.

Professional Imagery

Photos capture more than moments; they capture the essence of you. Thanks to our celebrity-obsessed culture, a professional photograph can elevate your perceived status. Such images paint you as a figure of importance, pushing aside the practicalities of how those photos came into existence. Aim for professional shots, but even high-quality photos taken from a well-angled smartphone can work wonders. Investing in this facet of personal branding is not just about aesthetics; it's about perception.

Harness the Power of Video

In the digital age, videos are the new television. When people see you on screen, it elevates your status to that of a television personality, granting you instant credibility. With easy access to platforms like Facebook Live and Instagram Stories, there's no reason not to embrace this medium. Videos foster connection and can increase your visibility, elevating your authority with each view.

Embrace Guest Expert Roles

Countless platforms are constantly on the hunt for guests to grace their stage – be it podcasts, Facebook communities or webinars. By finding your niche and presenting yourself as an authority in a specific domain, you become irresistible to these platforms. Moreover, your appearances become valuable digital assets, amplifying your online authority. As your expertise becomes recognized, more invitations will flood in, leading to collaborations, speaking engagements, and exponential audience growth.

Authority Drops

Sometimes it's the subtle cues that resonate the loudest. Mentioning a recent client success, a notable event you spoke at, or even a casual encounter with someone influential, can significantly boost your credibility. These 'authority drops' should be seamless and natural, subtly reminding your audience of your credentials without sounding boastful.

Qualifications and Accreditation

If you're an accredited coach, that's a badge of honour and a beacon of trust. Being affiliated with a renowned programme or institution lends you credibility, assuring clients of your expertise. Accreditation not only speaks of your competence but also boosts the confidence of potential clients in your ability to guide them.

6. Approach

Having journeyed deep into the realm of self-awareness, clarity and connection, you've forged a distinct identity in the world of coaching. As a beacon of enlightenment, you've sent out ripples of influence, nurturing an audience that resonates with your wisdom – but now it's time to turn a follower into a client, and sometimes that will require you to approach prospective clients and invite them to work with you.

The Symphony of Exchange

Sales, in the most profound sense of the word, are the heart's rhythm, a dance of souls seeking alignment. It's not just about business metrics; it's an affirmation of the value you infuse into lives. Your offerings aren't mere advice; they're the essence of your life's journey, wisdom and purpose. In return, what you receive isn't just financial compensation but a testament to the transformative power you wield. Life, in all its complexity, thrives on genuine exchange. Every dream your clients harbour, every obstacle they face, holds an invitation for you. An invitation to step in, to guide, to transform. When they invest in you, it's not just a purchase; it's an acknowledgement of a journey they wish to embark upon with you.

Conversations That Ignite the Soul

Engage in dialogues that are more than mere exchanges. Let them be revelations. Spark conversations that dive into their soul – their fears, dreams and aspirations. Offer them more than solutions; offer them visions of what could be. With every word, every anecdote, every piece of advice, you're not just communicating; you're weaving magic, crafting a tapestry of trust and possibility. The epitome of this journey is the discovery call. This isn't just a call; it's a sanctuary of mutual discovery. It's where reservations melt away, where dreams gain wings, and where partnerships are forged. Remember that every conversation, every discovery call, every connection, is a step towards you becoming a respected authority in the coaching industry. With every soul you touch, every life you transform, you don't just earn a client; you birth a legacy.

So, after all this you find yourself sitting in front of someone who's very interested in what you have to offer. They know, like and trust you, and you know exactly how to help them. Now I want to share how to structure the perfect discovery session . . .

Research, Relate and Respect

Find out a little bit about who you'll be speaking to ahead of time. Read their social media timelines, look at their pictures and go on their website if they have one. It doesn't need to take longer than a few minutes, but even just knowing a few snippets of information can help you to build a rapport. And just like when you go for an interview, show that you've done your research. They want to see that you know about them, that you've taken an interest in them and that they're not just a number to you. It's important that they feel like you have a genuine interest in supporting and helping them.

Build a Rapport, Share Your Story and
Set Expectations

Kick off the call by building a rapport – think of it as setting the stage. Introduce yourself, lay down the ground rules, and ensure they're crystal-clear about the hierarchy – you're the coach here, and you'll be steering this ship. Try starting with something along these lines: 'Hey there! Thanks for locking in this discovery call. We've chatted briefly through messages, but nothing beats a genuine conversation. Let's dive deep into how I can potentially help you and see if we're on the same wavelength to collaborate. Here's the game plan: we'll start with brief intros, then dive into a bit of coaching. If there's synergy, we'll discuss what a transformative twelve-week coaching experience with you might look like.' A structured start ensures the conversation isn't just a random chit-chat that doesn't culminate in a fruitful outcome.

Now, moving on to building that rapport. I reckon you've got this in the bag, but sometimes the basics work best. Did you know that in Britain, we chat about the weather on average seven times a day? We're naturals at this small talk game, so tap into that! After a bit of light banter, it's time for intros. This is your moment to shine! Share your journey, your achievements, and why you're the real deal in the coaching world. Remember, at this point, you may be an enigma to them, so it's good to establish your credibility. You're not just selling a service; you're selling your brand, your essence. They need to resonate with who you are because, ultimately, they're investing in you.

People predominantly make choices based on gut feelings and then use reason to justify those decisions. Share a snippet of your story, a glimpse into what made you take up coaching. Make it compelling, personal. Allow them to feel that intrinsic connection, and they're more likely to believe that partnering with you is the right move.

Unearth Crucial Information

Navigating sales boils down to a simple principle: understanding. The more you dig, the clearer the roadmap to closing the deal becomes. Begin by probing the basics. What's drawn them to seek coaching? What challenges are they up against? Then delve deeper into the nuances of your particular service. If it's about mindset transformation, ask pointedly: *What's holding you back? What doubts cloud your mind? What's sapping your drive?*

Understanding their pain points is pivotal. While everyone enjoys the allure of pleasure, it's pain that's the real motivator. Sure, we all chase joy, but it's not always the potent push we need to take action. Real change isn't spurred by mere wants; it's ignited by necessity, by the urge to escape discomfort.

This philosophy is mirrored in buying behaviour. If you can pinpoint their pain, diagnose their dilemma and present yourself as the remedy, you're gold. If the weight of their anguish eclipses the cost, they'll invest. But don't stop there. Dive into their aspirations, their goals and their dreams. Discuss every goal, from dealing with their immediate issues to facilitating their ultimate vision. By understanding both their pain and their passion, you're positioning yourself not just as a solution but as a bridge to a brighter future.

Sample Session: Showcase Your Expertise

Once you've concluded your detailed fact-finding segment, you realize you're not merely holding a set of data points. Instead, you're clutching a treasure trove of personal insights, waiting to be turned into a compelling narrative that can sway decisions. Begin by zeroing in on the tailored solutions that your service offers, specific to the challenges or aspirations they've shared. These insights give you an edge, allowing you to offer customized advice rather than generic solutions. The power of personalization can't be stressed enough, as nobody appreciates a one-size-fits-all solution.

Next, pivot subtly to a coaching stance. Even though it's essentially a sales call, this is your golden chance to introduce them to a real-life slice of your coaching techniques. Whether it's guiding them through a quick visualization tailored to their pain point, or a mental exercise that offers a glimmer of clarity, you should provide them with an authentic taste of how transformative a full session could be.

But your journey with them doesn't end with techniques and tactics. Dive into the power of narratives by sharing a part of your personal journey. Recount a moment, perhaps a challenge, a triumph, or even a lesson from a setback. The aim is not just to impress, but to forge a genuine connection. Real stories, laden with emotions and genuine experiences, have a unique way of bridging divides and drawing parallels.

Personalize Your Offering

So, you've showcased what you bring to the table, and if all has gone as planned, they've got a clear picture of the value you offer. The next step? Presenting the chance to dive deeper with you. Remember, customization is key. Each client is a unique individual with distinct needs. After your thorough chat during the fact-finding phase, you've got the insights needed to personalize your approach. Sure, you've got a structured coaching plan, but there's always space to weave in elements tailored just for them. You've gathered information about their aspirations and concerns; now it's time to align your offerings accordingly. Imagine saying, 'Joe, based on our conversation, I've structured a programme that aligns perfectly with what you're seeking.' Who could possibly turn that down?

You may say, 'Now, let's delve into the details. In my twelve-week programme, I start with a 2.5-hour breakthrough session. It's a powerful introduction that primes you for the journey ahead.' And as you outline the rest of your offerings, be descriptive. Paint a vivid picture: 'Every week, we'll engage in focused sessions. We'll navigate through those pivotal questions, ensuring you gain valuable self-insights.'

The true value lies in referencing their shared goals and concerns. If they're keen on building confidence, emphasize that. Say something like, 'Our sessions will zero in on bolstering your confidence, ensuring you're empowered in your business endeavours, consistently setting and achieving goals.' If they've highlighted motivation, address that too. 'As we progress, there'll be a shift towards sparking that intrinsic motivation within you. We'll uncover the core of your drive.'

Always circle back to their initial input, demonstrating that this isn't some generic package; it's a curated experience, designed especially for them.

Articulate the Value and Ask

It's crucial to stand firm in the value you provide. After discussing the specifics, confidently state your price: 'For the entire twelve-week programme – which includes the 2.5-hour break-through session, the weekly interactions, and all the dedicated work behind the scenes to ensure your success – it's priced at $1,000.' State your price clearly and pause. Let it sink in. Avoid the temptation to fill the silence. If they're contemplating, a gentle nudge like 'How does that sound to you?' can prompt a response.

It's common to hear 'I need to think about it'. Instead of letting it slide, engage further: 'I completely respect your need to reflect. Is there a specific aspect you're uncertain about? I'm here to address any questions or concerns you might have.' This encourages them to share any genuine reservations.

If the price seems to be a stumbling block, first underscore the value they'll be receiving. Consider this as a chance to coach them in recognizing the transformative potential of your coaching experience. Encourage them to view this as an investment rather than an expenditure. Remember, for many, it's about prioritizing. Help them see the value in their personal or business growth. If affordability remains a concern, be prepared to suggest flexible payment options. But always introduce these as alternatives, not as your primary offering. For instance, you could propose, 'I understand budget constraints. How about a three-month plan at $347 per month? Does that work better for you?' Continue to engage with their concerns. Every hesitation they voice is an opportunity for you to understand and address what's holding them back. If they express fear or uncertainty, empathize and reassure: 'It's natural to have reservations. I've been there too. Just know that I'll be here, supporting you every step of the way.'

Persist in the conversation, keeping their best interests at heart. Remember, you're not just aiming for a sale – you're looking to make a genuine impact on their lives. They've approached you, signalling their openness to what you offer. For many, a persuasive conversation is reassuring. It signifies passion, dedication, and belief in the service provided. So, be genuine, address their concerns, and help them see the transformative potential in partnering with you.

Embracing Your Worth When Asking for Payment

Charging for coaching? It's quite straightforward: you provide your rate, and that's it. The truth is, many have the means and recognize the value in what you offer. The real hurdle? It's your own self-imposed barriers, stemming from that little voice whispering, 'Are you truly worth that much?' Let me answer that for you: absolutely, you are. When you offer transformative coaching, it's not just about a chat. It's an exchange. They have a need; you have a skill. Money becomes the universally accepted token of this value swap. It's not some intricate dance; it's merely matching one desire with another.

Think about it: whether you're asking for $1 or $10,000 an hour, they're still hitting the jackpot. What they hand you is essentially a number on a screen or a printed piece of paper – a symbolic token. In places like the UK, our banknotes even declare 'I promise to pay the bearer on demand the sum of . . .' – reinforcing that money is essentially an IOU. But what you bring to the table is tangible: it's authentic value.

Your coaching encompasses years of dedication, expertise, trials, errors, wisdom, and the gift of time. While money can always be earned, time is irreversible. It's the planet's most precious commodity, one not even the wealthiest can buy back. Every coaching session carves out a piece of your life, supplemented by the even larger chunk you've already devoted to honing your craft.

So when you ponder over your price tag, don't get sidetracked by competitors or client expectations. Remember, you're not just a commodity; you're a unique blend of experiences and skills. While the idea of plucking a number from the ether might feel uncomfortable, trust that there's someone willing to match it. Sure, not everyone will be onboard, but remember that time is finite, and you can only take on so many clients. It's okay to be selective.

Consider this: with nearly 8 billion individuals worldwide, recent data from Business Insider highlights an astonishing 46.8 million millionaires. Beyond this elite group, imagine the countless others enjoying comfortable six-figure salaries, with a plush bank balance ready for the right investment. Many might possess financial wealth but are grappling with emotional or personal challenges, yearning for guidance or a fresh direction. To them, their bank balance is just a number. The real value? The potential transformation through coaching – and that's where you shine.

Money is merely a tool, a means to an end. But your life, your expertise, your time? It's incomparably more valuable. So step up with confidence, recognize your worth, and present your fees like you're offering them the steal of the century. Because, quite frankly, you are.

Navigating the 'Salesy' Stigma

At its heart, sales isn't about pushing products; it's about forging genuine connections. It's about delivering something of value that people want and bringing them to a place where they're eager for more. Instead of trying to force-feed products, concentrate on those people who genuinely resonate with what you offer. Think of it as a mutual exchange – you're sharing your expertise, experiences and time, and in return they offer financial appreciation. Life is a two-way street: 'What can I bring to your table, and what can you bring to mine?' Some might be wrestling with personal challenges or chasing big dreams. By helping them navigate these, it's only fair to receive compensation for your time and expertise.

Selling, understandably, can feel daunting. It's like standing at a crossroads where one path leads to acceptance and the other to rejection. With every sale, you either strike gold or come up empty-handed, making the process feel incredibly binary: success or failure, win or lose. But rather than dwelling on the pressures, remember that every outcome is a learning opportunity. You're understanding your customers better, honing your pitch, and gauging what resonates. Each 'no' today is a step closer to a 'yes' tomorrow. My suggestion for those starting out? Embrace the challenge. Instead of hunting for instant yeses, seek the noes. They're the true gold mines of learning. And who knows? In the process of chasing those noes, you might just land a client or two!

It's not uncommon for coaches to grapple with their own insecurities when it comes to sales. Maybe you question your worth, or doubt your skills, or perhaps the thought of a 'yes' feels more intimidating than a 'no'. Maybe you're unsure about your niche or whether you'll vibe with a potential client. Such uncertainties can make you pull punches, skip pitches or even dodge client interactions. But here's a nugget of advice from me: push past the hesitations and dive right in. When you witness firsthand the transformative impact you have on your clients, those initial hesitations about selling will vanish.

But to witness that change, you've got to take that first step. Remember, regardless of any sale's outcome, you're invaluable. Rejections or failures don't define you. Think of the amazing mentors who've shaped lives – like that prison tutor or rehab counsellor who turned mine around. If they'd let their fears hold them back, I'd still be lost. They earned every penny for the profound change they sparked in me. And you, with the invaluable service you offer, have a similar power to bring about change.

Many might be too hesitant or unfamiliar with coaching to ask for help outright. They need you to reach out and to build that bridge. Your service is a beacon. You're not just selling coaching; you're offering transformation. Don't deny them, or yourself, that chance.

Becoming a life coach isn't just a career move – it's a declaration of freedom. This book has shown you how to stop seeing your struggles as scars and start using them as stepping stones. Life coaching is the ultimate expression of that transformation – the moment you turn your personal pain into a professional superpower. It's not about perfection. It's not about having all the answers. It's about being real, being raw, and being ready to help someone else rise because you've been there too.

This is more than a strategy. This is your turning point. And when you pair the power of coaching with the depth of your own lived experience, you don't just build a business – you build a movement. This is how you turn adversity into a tangible asset and how you become truly unlimited – for you and for the rest of the world.